GI LIMEY

A Welsh-American in WWII

Clifford Guard was born in 1923, in the south Wales city of Swansea. When WWII broke out, he joined the US Army's 3rd Armored Division, where he was nicknamed 'Limey'. He has received multiple awards for his bravery in combat. After several decades living in the U.S., he returned to Swansea at age sixty-two and still resides there today.

Geraint Thomas is a Swansea Valley-based writer and journalist. A graduate of the Cardiff School of Journalism (2002), he also gained an MA in Creative and Media Writing from Swansea University (2006). Having worked on the *South Wales Evening Post* for sixteen years he became a freelance writer in 2018. To date he has had seven books published and seen two of his plays (*After Milk Wood* and *Roofless*) performed professionally. In the past Geraint has been shortlisted for News Reporter of the Year in the 2016 Wales Media Awards and one of his previous works, *Terry Davies - Wales's First Superstar Fullback*, was shortlisted for the Cross Sports Book Awards in 2017. Geraint Thomas also does stand up comedy and hates cycling.

GI LIMEY

A Welsh-American in WWII

Clifford Guard
with Geraint Thomas

Parthian, Cardigan SA43 1ED
www.parthianbooks.com
First published in 2019
© Clifford Guard with Geraint Thomas 2019
ISBN 978-1-912109-02-9
Editor: Edward Matthews
Cover design: www.theundercard.co.uk
Typeset by Elaine Sharples
Printed by 4edge Limited
Published with the financial support of the Welsh Books Council.
British Library Cataloguing in Publication Data
A cataloguing record for this book is available from the British Library.

This book is dedicated to all the brave men I served alongside in the Second World War—especially Ralph 'Trixie' Trinkley and Henry 'The Greek' Kallas—and in commemoration of all the true heroes who never made it home, including General Maurice Rose, a real soldier's soldier.

Foreword

Clifford Guard first entered my consciousness in August 2011 when I was handed a copy of a feature from the US-based *Muskegon Chronicle* called 'Limey, Trix and The Greek', which detailed how the friendship of three close buddies helped them through some of the Second World War's bloodiest campaigns.

Just over a year later I met him in person when I was asked to report on the unveiling of a plaque commemorating those American troops who were stationed in Swansea ahead of the D-Day landings. I shook his hand and asked if I could write his life story.

For the next two years most Sundays saw me making my way down to Mumbles to sit with Clifford, in his room overlooking the sea for an hour or so, listening to him unpick a life as far removed from the ordinary as they come. Seldom did I fail to be moved and humbled through listening to this modest old soldier recalling the exploits that saw him and his pals freely risk their lives in the name of democracy and freedom.

What has been impossible to replicate on these pages are the haunted looks, silent tears and painful pauses where Clifford has been lost in far off moments that have not dwindled down the years — just think back to traumatic times in your own life and you will understand how, sadly, some of his experiences have been far too easily recalled.

Clifford speaks bluntly at times about his thoughts and feelings and uses the vocabulary of a soldier on the line, however, he is merely telling it like it was back in the day. The reader needs to realise this rather than take offence; any derogatory comments are directed at those who were trying to kill him.

It is important to state that *GI Limey* is not a history book but the memoir of a ninety-two-year-old retired US soldier and while every effort has been made to ensure it is factually correct the reader must realise that Clifford has reached back over seventy years in recalling much of his narrative, so please forgive any inconsistencies. That said, his service and the battles he fought in are a matter of public record and Clifford stands by his testimony. I do not doubt the word of someone who has built his entire life upon the foundations of honour, truth and duty.

Throughout the whole process of writing this book Clifford has maintained that he is no hero. 'The real heroes never came home' he recalls with sadness. Commendable words but I also class Clifford Guard a hero — he freely placed his life on the line for the freedom we often take for granted today and while, fortunately, he did not fall in battle, he has carried the torment inside ever since.

Read his story and make up your own mind, but I for one salute the man who I am privileged to have been able to come to call my buddy, and thank him for his service.

Geraint Thomas

Prologue

Off Omaha Beach, June 23, 1944 Spearhead US Army 3rd Armored Division

Our landing craft hit the beach at the break of dawn. My squad had been ordered into our half-track, in the belly of that vessel, half an hour or so before. There was no talking; everyone was dead quiet, no doubt saying a silent prayer or two. I was alone up in the turret with only its .50 calibre machine gun for company; the other guys were down in the well. We could hear the roar of the artillery, coming from the battleships behind us, and shells racing overhead to zero-in on the area above the beach, which was now the killing ground. I thought to myself, 'What in hell can we expect when we land?' I was pretty numb and somewhat disorientated.

We were at full speed going in, around twelve knots, because with two dozen or so half-tracks and tanks on board we weighed close to five thousand tonnes and it was important that the nose of that craft nudged as far up the beach as possible to avoid the wet sand, which would bog the vehicles down. I can still remember the shudder as she hit and we knew there and then that, after eighteen months of hard training, this was it.

When those huge bow doors opened up I could see a slab of menacing sky, slated with rain, with streaks of early light trying to break through the gloom—the weather, even in June, had been so damned terrible we had spent the best part of two days waiting off the coast for it to settle down enough to allow us to go in. It was bitterly cold but I didn't really feel it, as I was too anxious. I was keyed up.

'This is the real thing,' I thought. 'I hope to God that I come out of this half-way decent.'

Looking back, if we had known what hell would visit us over the next eleven months or so, and the price we would pay for meeting it head on, I doubt we would have driven onto that beach. But we had signed up to the US Army determined to put a stop to the evil which was raging against the world. There would be no going back until we had finished the job that lay ahead and too many of us would never see home again.

Chapter 1

A Swansea Boy

I was born across the Pond in the United Kingdom, in September 1923, within an artillery barrage of another large expanse of sand on the shores of south-west Wales, in the coastal town of Swansea, into a far different battle where the struggle to survive was not as pronounced but still one that some lost; if you were poor at least.

Back then Wales, one of the four countries which make up the United Kingdom, was a very impoverished place as far as I was concerned because I was born on the lowest rung of the socioeconomic ladder. That's where I was and I'm proud of it in a way because it motivated me to really get on in life.

I grew up during the time of the Great Depression and General Strike, when people became poor and hungry across the planet. We were hit particularly hard in our own little corner of the world as Swansea had dragged itself up on the back of our industries but the order books had dried up and working class people paid the price. It's just the way that the country was. To me, growing up, it seemed as though Swansea was in a permanent slump.

My father, William Guard, was a labourer; that's all he had to offer, his strong arms and strong back to do hard manual graft. He was unemployed for a large part of my childhood, so odd jobs kept us going as a family. He would go down to the docks to try to get a day's work but there would always be a whole load of other guys standing around looking for work too. Swansea was a mighty hard place to live. There was just no work around. It wasn't like today with a culture where people choose to live on benefits; back then, if you didn't earn a wage you starved.

As a kid I remember going with my father down to the back of the YMCA and he would stand in line to draw the dole—the small allowance paid to the unemployed. It's vivid in my memory. I would stand quietly next to him as he'd smoke a hand-rolled cigarette. His flat cap would be pulled down over his head and he'd wear a muffler. Sometimes it used to rain and I would watch the water running off his cap.

He would talk to the fellas in front and behind him in the line; they would all be puffing their smokes. Then, when we reached the front, he had to sign a book and he got something like thirty shillings (around £2 or $3), which he handed over to my mother to last the whole family the week.

*

My mother's maiden name was Annie Sullivan. She had a good brain on her but came from a very poor Irish family. True to her Emerald Isle roots she had religion and I had a strict Catholic upbringing. I didn't mind going to church but I didn't know what it was all about, I couldn't understand much of it because it was in Latin. Even today I'm not a churchgoing man, although I do believe in a higher power.

*

I was the first-born of five brothers: Alfie, David, Henry, Alan and John, and three sisters: Edwina, Eunice and Margaret.

Swansea's most famous son, Dylan Thomas, may have written fondly of growing up in his little sea town on the long and splendid-curving shore; but he was the son of the grammar school's English master and lived in suburbia with a cook and a maid. We always lived in a hovel with sticks of furniture and a bed of straw. We children slept on a heap of straw sewn into two old blankets but no sheets.

We had no running water inside the house, just a tap outside, so if you wanted water you would get a bucket and fill it up. As for toilets, we had to go out the back, and we used a newspaper for toilet paper.

We lived in quite a number of places in Swansea as money was tight and the rent would often go unpaid.

The debt would build until eventually my mother would wake us kids in the middle of the night and tell us to get up, she didn't say pack your things because we didn't have much of anything, and we would be gone; Houdini had nothing on my family.

*

Before I had reached the age of ten, home-life was to undergo change in a huge way. My dad sat me down one day and said, 'Your mother and I are splitting up, and we are going to get a divorce.'

At the time, I didn't know what a divorce was, I was too young to understand and it was quite rare back then. My parents had initially got along well but apparently when my mother met Arthur, my father's brother, she fell in love with him, and then there was a divorce.

My mother married Arthur and took us kids with her. My dad later married a woman called Elsie, who was one fine lady. The brothers settled their differences but were never really close. In a sense, growing up, I had two dads.

*

Sadly, I am no stranger to death, having witnessed the bloodied beaches and battlefields of Normandy, before advancing across the carnage of Nazi-occupied Europe, but I was no more than a boy when I first knew loss.

My little sister, Eunice, died when she was a baby. It was so long ago but I think that she died of diphtheria, a respiratory disease all but eradicated in the Western world today, but at the time it was a real killer which was linked to overcrowded and unhygienic living conditions; not very pleasant, but that was the world we lived in back then.

When she became sick Eunice was taken away to the Swansea Union Workhouse, which was near the top of the town in an area called Mount Pleasant. Despite its name it was not a pleasant place, but when families couldn't cope—as when Eunice was sick—that's where you ended up.

All I can remember is a little coffin coming back with my sister inside when she passed away. She was barely twelve months old. It was a terrible thing to have to go through. It really did my mother in. I don't recall the funeral; I can't even tell you today where she is laid to rest.

My next sister, Edwina, and I, nearly suffered the same fate when we also caught diphtheria. We were in hospital for about four months; I can still remember the smell of the disinfectant. The nurses wore hats and starched aprons and moved about very quickly and business-like, yet they were great with the children.

That was, in fact, a feature with the medical profession during my childhood. The doctors would come into your home and sit down and have a cup of tea. They were family-orientated back then; they would come in and check on the whole family. They would recognise the poverty and were very kind and very understanding, especially with us children.

My brother was also institutionalised at one point, due to his health. Little Alfie had a disability; his legs were weak so he couldn't use them. He lived with us up until the age of ten but then he went to live in a Catholic-run children's home called Nazareth House because my Mam wasn't able to care for him; I loved him.

Later in life he became fairly well known in Swansea because he used to sell the *Evening Post* newspaper down by the market. He used to sit on a little stool down there and holler out, 'Evening Post!' Everybody knew Alfie Guard.

At one point as a kid, I too worked for the newspaper, selling it at the bottom of Townhill. I would catch the men going to their jobs in the docks. I used to get up at six in the morning and go down to the paper's offices and they would give me a sack of Posts and off I would go. It wasn't much but it was all money coming in for my Mam.

Swansea today is almost unrecognisable from the town of my childhood thanks to the Luftwaffe (the German air force) bombing the crap out of it during the war, but when I delve into my memories it comes back to me.

At the heart of town you had the fancy Ben Evans

department store on one side of the street and its competitor, David Evans, on the other. Opposite them was the relic of Swansea Castle and the *Evening Post* building near Castle Buildings, where the posh people lived above a row of tailor shops and bakeries.

It was all trams back then. They were electric, powered by overhead cables, and they came right through Swansea, all the way from a suburb called Cwmbwrla in the north, straight down High Street, past the Palace Theatre and train station, into the town centre with a junction near the two Evans stores branching off right down Oxford Street, towards the market and onto the General Hospital, while, carrying straight on, you would go down Wind Street towards the old Seamen's Mission and the sea.

We couldn't afford to pay to go on the trams, however, there was another way for us kids. The trams had a big light on the back and the front and, if we were going anywhere, we used to latch on to them and sit on the back to get a free ride. Of course the conductors knew that the kids did this, and they could get pretty nasty. They would sometimes have a rope and they would flick it at you to make you get off as the tram was moving.

Being built up on the banks of the River Tawe, where it meets the sea, Swansea was a natural port and it dominated the town. There were several docks, one of which was in the Strand, behind Wind Street (the River Tawe used to flow a different route back then) and you would be able to see the masts of the tall ships rising above the buildings when you walked down the street.

Lower Wind Street, bearing in mind that Swansea was a sailors' town, was a den of iniquity. Down the bottom you had the arches, which carried the railway, and there you would find gambling, prostitution, drinking, all sorts of vice; but no drugs, these didn't come on the scene until years later.

*

I used to know all those streets like the back of my hand and it felt as though they belonged to my pals and me. Like all kids I had a gang of close friends growing up, who were like my first squad of GIs, as we all looked out for each other. There were four of us altogether: myself, Billy Jones, Tommy McCarthy and Charlie Blanco. None of us came from well-to-do backgrounds, although I guess I was the poorest, but you don't really think along those lines as a kid. We were all about the same age and size but I was the boss and kept everyone in line.

We all had our own skills, as it were. Tommy McCarthy was quite good at picking locks, Billy Jones was a tough guy and very handy when it came to mixing it up with the gangs from the rougher Strand or Greenhill areas of the town (when I say gangs, it wasn't the sort with knives and guns you see today, it was just kids being kids), Charlie Blanco was one hell of a sweet talker, he could get things done, and I was a little more cheeky and aggressive than the lot, always the first to climb over a wall or to speak my mind.

*

Now, being poor, food was hard to come by; we ate when we could. If we had bread and jam on the table then we were really eating! People can't take that in today but that was the way it was. We had a coal fire and there was a swinging iron arm from which our Mam would hang a big pot that she used to boil up vegetables and whatever scraps of meat we could get our hands on.

I'm not proud to say it but my buddies and I sometimes resorted to pinching food. With my Catholic background it didn't sit easy on my conscience but we never thought about it as stealing. It wasn't like shoplifting today; we did it out of absolute necessity. People may take umbrage over it but I'm telling you like it was, it was a direct result of the poverty. We didn't do it because we were naughty but because it was essential.

At the time Swansea had the biggest and grandest indoor market around, with hundreds of stalls selling everything from potatoes to peas and chickens to seabass. It ran for a whole block along Oxford Street and it had the most ornate of entrances, with two domed towers either side of large, twenty-foot-high iron gates. Sadly, the old market failed to survive the war. German incendiary bombs smashed through its massive glass roof, leaving the whole building a twisted wreck of metal and burnt-out debris.

There were no trucks back then, just little vans and lots of horses and carts that used to take all the goods inside the market. Over time they had worn ruts into the cobbles. I was nothing but skin and bones and I found that I could use the ruts to scoot under the gate. Of course, it would be closed at the time and all the stores would be covered up with cloth. The danger was the night watchman walking around inside, so I was quiet as a mouse and learned to take a handful of vegetables—the meat would be all locked up—and hurry them home to Mam and she would throw them into that big pot.

We also stole to keep the fire going. One of my aunts lived in St Thomas, to the east of the town, and we used to go over there and climb down a big, steep embankment into a railway yard, to where the coal was stored. We used to scoot down with these old sacks that they used to keep onions or potatoes in, fill them up, just as much as you could carry, and take them back up the slope and hide the haul in my aunt's front garden before going back down for more.

We learnt to be very quiet because they had railway police who, if they caught you, would give you a real beating.

*

We would come up with no end of ways to beg or steal in order to survive. For instance, there was no central heating, it was all coal, and even the bedrooms had little fireplaces, so that presented an opportunity. We would go down to the market, when it was open this time, and get orange boxes, which were made out of wood, and smash them up and tie the pieces up into little bundles. We would then go around the houses, knocking on doors, to sell them as kindling to start the fires.

Another trick was to go down to the railway yard where they used to park up the wagons in the sidings. We would climb over a stone wall, run across the line, and there would be stockpiles of empty beer bottles. We would pinch as many as we could carry. We would get a penny a bottle by taking them back to public houses in the town. We had to be cute about it, mind you, and not go to the same place too often, as we didn't want to draw attention to ourselves. If I made three pence I would give that to Mam and we could have bread.

Then we used to go down to South Dock where you found the town's fish market. The trawlers used to come in and unload their catch there. Many times I would go down there with Billy Jones, Tommy McCarthy and Charlie Blanco and say, 'Hey mister, can I have a fish for Mam, please?'

The fishermen knew how tough things were. They would ask, 'How many brothers and sisters have you got?'

When I replied, they said, 'Okay then, you can have a big fish.'

Elsewhere in town, near to the Castle Cinema, was a lane which ran along the back of some shops, which included a couple of bakeries. We used to knock on their back doors, once they had closed, and they would get rid of all the stuff they hadn't sold during the day. For two pennies you got some leftover bread, perhaps some stale cakes and custard slices; it all helped.

*

Despite our obvious poverty we never really felt that we were poor and the posh kids never acted posh, we wouldn't stand for that. And while nearly all my friends were in the same boat and came from poor backgrounds, I did get to see how the other half lived on occasions.

There was one kid, in our wider group, whose father was an attorney. I was invited to his home in the Uplands area, which was made up of big houses and villas. They had a switch to turn on the light—we didn't even have electricity. I remember looking at it and wishing that I had one of those in my house.

His mother said, 'Why don't you take Clifford upstairs and show him your room?'

We went up and played for a while. Then she came upstairs and told us to come down and have some Welsh cakes. It was amazing to go into their kitchen and see all their food.

I can remember vividly asking her, 'Can I have more than one Welsh cake?'

'Yes,' she said, 'you can have more than one Welsh cake and you can have more than one glass of milk, if you want it.'

Her husband, a very stern-looking man, was sat by the fire reading a book. The fire was well banked and it was real big. He just looked at me—a snotty-nosed kid with one sock hanging out of a hole in my shoe and the other hanging down. It wasn't a very pleasant look.

But the mother was very kind. She said, and I can remember her words to this day, 'When you are passing, Clifford, be sure to come in and say hello.'

*

At Christmas we used to get metal bands off barrels and interweave them until they made a big ball and we would wrap paper around it and, with pieces of cotton thread, hang sweets from it. We used to put our socks on the mantelpiece and when we woke up in the morning there would be some nuts, an apple and usually some dates in them. Toys were made out of wood. My father was quite skilled and he would carve different things, like a cradle and doll for my sisters or a boat for us boys. It was a joyous occasion. We actually thought Santa had come and done this. We thoroughly believed in Santa Claus.

*

The beaches in and around Swansea were well visited in those days; there wasn't much else for working-class people to do that was free. On bank holidays, in particular, we would go down the beach as a family. We used to take jam sandwiches and sugar pop (made by mixing sugar with water). We had a whale of a time down there. Occasionally my aunty would have some chocolate and we kids were entitled to a piece; it was pretty much a rarity.

We used to play football on the sand and run around chasing each other, ending up splashing in the tide. The water was absolutely clean. We never talked about pollution in those days, because the sea was sparkling clean. It was a time of happiness.

The gentry, the men in their sharp suits and the ladies with long frocks and parasols, would go for a stroll along the promenade and I can remember staring at them as they climbed out of their automobiles. It was like they were from another world.

Some people used to catch the train down to Mumbles, a popular fishing village at the far end of the bay. Sometimes my gang and I would sneak on that train, as boys do, and have a good time. Often we would end up on Mumbles Pier and dive off into the water. I used to love swimming and diving. We would also get a hook and dangle it on some line in the water; I don't know why we bothered because we never caught a darn thing.

To us poor kids the cinema was usually out of the question but we came up with a good scam to get in almost for free. We would scrape together the odd penny and halfpenny between the members of the gang and pool it altogether to buy a ticket. Usually I would go in on my own and, when the lights went down, I would go down the front, where there was a corridor behind the screen, and open a door to let all the boys in. Sometimes, when I opened that door, there would be up to twelve guys waiting, yet there were only four in my gang.

I remember one time I did this and on our way back to the seats I heard a voice, 'Clifford, what are you doing?' My mother was sitting in the third row.

'Nothing, Mam, just watching the film with the boys.'

'You sneaked in, didn't you?'

'Yes, Mam.'

'Well you behave yourself or else I will tell the manager.'

*

On a few rare occasions my father took me to see a movie. On one trip, to the Carlton Cinema, on Oxford Street (it's a Waterstones bookshop today) they were showing a film about the American Army and that was the first time that I saw the Yankee uniforms. My father told me on a number of occasions, 'Son, if you ever get to America, stay there, it's the land of opportunity; if you work hard enough you can get ahead. If you stay here you will never get to secondary school, you won't be able to get a good education and make something of your life.'

His words stuck in my mind.

*

There wasn't the level of social care around that there is today but one thing that kept me on the straight and narrow—probably saved my life—was my membership of the town's Boys' Club.

There were around eighty boys of all ages and we would meet up most days in the old Gospel Mission, behind the central police station in Orchard Street. It was open all the time, except for Sundays, from around four in the afternoon until around ten at night.

Mr Hopkins, who ran the place, was a father figure to us. He had served in the army and he had a tremendous effect on us all. If we pinched anything and he found out, or you were caught out lying, you would get such a dressing down. I have always tried to be honest with people; I got that from the Boys' Club. I cannot abide the distortion of the truth; truth, for me, is what I fought for.

And Mr Hopkins's wife was a real Welsh Mam to us all. Every once in a while, she would bring in a tray of sandwiches to feed us. Then at Christmas time they would present you with a basket of fruit.

I used to spend a lot of time down the Boys' Club chatting to my pals and playing billiards, but they also had a basement where we could do gymnastics, which Mr Hopkins loved to teach.

I also learnt how to box in that basement. I wasn't outstanding but I was good and I could take a punch. We used to go up and box the guys in the valleys. It was one of the rare occasions we would travel by bus. It was just three rounds, as we were only kids, but I enjoyed it. And while I didn't go looking for trouble I used my skills to take care of my brothers and sisters; nobody messed with them.

The Swansea Boys' Club even helped to fit us out with clothes. The winters were really harsh. They used to call us snotty-nosed kids in those days because we had icicles hanging from our nostrils. Sometimes you would have odd socks on and your clothes weren't very warm but the Boys' Club knew what was going on and they gave us coats and boots.

There was a wonderful lady, by the name of Aeron Thomas, who took an interest in the welfare of the boys in the Swansea Boys' Club. Her husband was into shipping and steel, and they were well off. She was a great influence on my life.

I remember one day she stopped me and looked down and said, 'How come you are wearing such bad shoes?' I had newspaper blocking up a hole in the sole.

I was lost for an answer. She added: 'I shall get you a pair of shoes.'

And she did. I became the proud owner of brand-new hobnailed boots.

It wasn't only Mrs Aeron Thomas. The whole of Swansea's business community were giving money, not a lot, but enough to make a real difference to the Boys' Club.

The club was also responsible for the first ever holiday of my life and it still ranks up there amongst the best. We had a lovely week at the Boys' Club of Wales's camp forty miles away in St Athan, near Cardiff. The journey itself was something else: the longest coach trip I had ever been on.

Once there they kept us busy by setting up sports, running and swimming. The club even provided us with a toothbrush, toothpaste and a bar of scented soap; I can still remember the smell. I didn't even have a toothbrush of my own at home—I had to share one with my siblings.

For some reason the police gave up their time and got involved. They used to instruct us in gymnastics and also gave us talks on a whole host of topics, from the universe to cities of the world.

The police presence was much greater in old Swansea

and its surrounding areas. The officers were stern but fair and helpful; I can't say enough good about them because if it weren't for their interest in the Swansea Boys' Club I don't know where I would have been today. They weren't doing it for show or presentation; they did it because they were genuinely interested in making sure young Swansea boys grew up on the straight and narrow, with proper guidance and understanding. They got involved from the top down.

Years later I wrote a letter to the chief of police in Swansea to thank them for giving me a chance in life.

*

Alongside the Boys' Club there was another institution that greatly affected my life—the Royal Naval Cadets. I first joined as a thirteen-year-old, but not for the right reasons.

One day Billy Jones said to me, 'Let's try to get into the Sea Cadets.'

I said, 'Why?'

He said, 'Well, if we put on that uniform the girls will chase us.'

'That's not a bad idea,' I replied, 'how do we go about this?'

'I don't know. We will ask Mr Hopkins.'

I loved the Sea Cadets and it helped kindle that burning desire to take to the sea one day. The hall where we used to meet was near St Mary's Church in the town centre. They taught us seamanship, how to tie knots, elementary navigation and citizenship – they even had a small boat in which they used to teach us to row in the docks. I thoroughly enjoyed it because we also had sports and boxing. But, best of all, they gave us a regular miniature navy uniform and a pair of boots.

Plenty of girls caught my eye but my standard dress wasn't really appropriate for the class that most of them came from, being a poor little Welsh boy, but, by golly, the uniform worked. When you were trying to make friends with a girl you were always on your best behaviour to show them that you were an okay kind of guy. You would laugh and joke and sometimes hold hands. You never tried to kiss a girl—it just wasn't done. You would just go for a walk, mainly to the park.

I was also with St John Ambulance for about a year because they, too, had a nice uniform. It also meant that I could get into places like the movies and the YMCA theatre for free.

*

As for my education, I attended St David's Catholic School, a two-storey building next to St David's Church in the town centre. It's a car park now. The downstairs housed the infants and the upstairs was home to the junior classrooms.

The headmaster, Mr Welsh, was a very stern man. When you went into school on Monday mornings he would be standing at the gate.

As I walked by he would ask, 'Clifford, did you go to church on Sunday?'

'Yes, Sir,' I would reply looking at the floor.

'Who was giving the sermon?' he would spot-check.

'The Reverend Kelly,' I would guess, knowing to look out if he found out I was lying to him, because he carried a stick.

I wasn't good academically because I didn't see the use of it. I didn't like reading unless it was *Boy's Own* kind of stuff, which I could identify with. I had difficulty in learning, difficulty with p and b, which I still do today. I now know that I have a form of dyslexia but it was unheard of in my time. I couldn't add 2 and 2 and come up with the right answer. And history—forget it—I wasn't the least bit interested in kings and queens. I was good in geography, though, which was put to good use in later years when I went out into the wider world.

I spent a lot of time standing in the corner with a dunce's hat on my head. It was a pointed hat and I wore it on numerous occasions. You were given it for not being quiet in class, being rude, for not taking your homework in when you should, and if you answered back to the teacher. There were many reasons and when I did them with consistency the teacher would say, 'Clifford, pick up the hat and go and stand in the corner.'

Now, when I had done that, Billy Jones, Charlie Blanco or Tommy McCarthy would get an elastic band and place it between thumb and forefinger and use it to flick paper darts at me.

Despite the discipline, we had some lovely teachers in St David's, very real and decent human beings. They were very strict but very kind, compassionate and understanding; they knew by the way we were dressed that we had it tough.

*

All things considered, as a child growing up in Swansea, I was kind of happy and accepted things for the way they were because I didn't know any different. I can honestly say that, even though we were very poor, people were sociable and would talk to you in the street or what have you – a lot of them were in the same boat. I loved the old Swansea Town.

What I didn't know, at the time, was that the values I had learnt, and the way things had shaped me as I strived to survive in that town, were to stand me in good stead for what was to become one heck of a journey through life, which would take me far away from that sandy shore to most corners of the world and through one of mankind's darkest and most violent hours.

Chapter 2

Life in the Merchant Navy

I guess you could say I was born with saltwater running through my veins. With Swansea having a rich maritime history I came from a long line of sailors, and as a boy, I loved nothing more than to run down to the docks and watch the ships coming in.

Swansea was still an important seaport during my childhood, even though the glory days when the town exported copper all around the world, were long gone. Now it was mostly coal, mined from the valleys, and tin plate. The railhead went down to the docks and loaded the waiting ships, while in reverse they had a lot of timber coming in from Norway, along with other goods from Europe, grain being one. The quaysides were full of cranes and warehouses.

I had always wanted to go to sea and my time in the Sea Cadets had only served to heighten my thirst for the adventure that it would bring. So when I left school, on the day before my fourteenth birthday, I was determined to chase my dream; but my mother had other ideas.

I said to her, 'I want to join the Royal Navy, Mam.'

'Definitely not,' she replied. She said that it was too dangerous and that my place was at home trying to help the family.

I thought to myself, 'We'll see.' I decided that I would go to sea one way or another; I'm the kind of individual who, if I set a goal, I will achieve it.

Forced to put my seafaring plans on hold, for the time being at least, and with secondary school firmly out of the question, as my family just didn't have the money, I looked for work.

Initially I got a job as an apprentice with the Welsh Glassworks, near St Mary's Church. I was with them for about six months and was taught how to do the piping for leaded lights. Then I worked for a wine company for a while, as a delivery boy with a bike with a basket on the front, until I almost lost a full load trying to get up Constitution Hill. It's practically a one in ten gradient. When I got back I told them I couldn't do it no more. My next job was in a shoe repair shop called SOS (Save Our Soles) on Wind Street.

I liked the world of work, and it was good to be earning, but my longing for the sea would not go away; fortunately I found an ally in my stepfather.

When I was fifteen he was on a merchant ship called the *Selvistan*. He worked down in the engine room, as a stoker. He was very strong. He was a good guy.

One day he arrived home with the exciting news that they needed a cabin boy.

My Mam was not happy but I told her that I would be able to send her money every week. That made her come around to the idea, along with the fact that my stepfather would be on the same ship to keep an eye on me. It also gave her the opportunity, for the first time in her life, to buy some half-decent furniture.

So, in May 1939, I found myself going down to the shipping company's office with my stepfather to sign up as a merchant seaman.

*

I will never forget that first morning, when I left my home and walked down the waking streets, with a duffle bag containing my belongings slung over my shoulder. It must have been six in the morning, still dark and very cold and drizzly; not very nice weather but I was on top of the world.

For a while I walked alongside a policeman who I knew from the Boys' Club. We came to a turning and, before he went the other way, he turned to me and said, 'Clifford, lots of luck.'

I can still trace that walk in my mind. I walked past the Palace Theatre, between the big David and Ben Evans stores, down Wind Street, turned left, past Weavers Flour Mill, over the swing bridge, past the Norwegian church, turned left again and went onto the ship.

The first thing that hit me was the reality of being on board such a big ship. She wasn't a modern vessel by any stretch, just an old tramp ship, a beat-up old gal with an engine that was kind of dicey, that takes cargo – but to me she was like the Queen Elizabeth cruise liner waiting to take me away from all the poverty and hardship of my childhood.

I felt happy as I stood on the deck and looked out over the rail of that ship, towards the town, as she left the docks, taking me on my first voyage. I scanned the beach where I used to run about as a kid, past the pier heads reaching out from the docks, and inland, searching out familiar landmark buildings, the tower of St Mary's Church, the tall twin pillars of the entrance to the indoor market and Weaver's Flour Mill, the places and people of my childhood slipping into the distance. And then I was sick.

Once my sea legs came I got stuck into the work. The job of a deck boy was to do whatever the ordinary seamen wanted you to do—folding ropes and being on hand in case help was needed. One task was holystoning, where you had to get on your knees and scrub the deck. You also had to chip off the old paint from the metalwork, with a steel brush, to make it ready to be repainted. Sometimes, while in port, this included being hauled down the side of the ship on a plank. Risk assessment and health and safety were unheard of back then.

That first voyage went over to France and Holland. I

was paid about ten shillings and it lasted a week. I wasn't homesick or anything like that because my stepdad was on board to take care of me as he always had.

*

The seamen were usually nice guys and they were helpful and quite friendly. There was one fella on that ship, however, who was a real mean sonofabitch. He was the bosun. He was a big man and he had muscles on him like a bunny running under a rug. He had a rope with a knot tied at the end that he used to carry under his belt, and he would use it to hit you if you weren't doing right. I didn't get hit much because I always used to do as I was told.

That didn't stop him picking on me and calling me stupid, though. Then he did give me a clout.

My stepdad wasn't big but he was wiry and he was fast. He got hold of this big fella and he beat the living daylights out of him.

Afterwards he said, 'You touch my son again and I will kill you.' I was okay from there on in.

*

My next voyage took me further afield, carrying coal all the way across the Atlantic to Montreal. The old tramp was able to do about ten knots and it took us around ten days to cross over. I had heard a lot about the Atlantic. My stepdad told me that it was a terrible place to sail, especially during the winter months.

The power of the Atlantic is unbelievable. The height of the waves was between ten to fourteen feet high on average. When the ship's bow hits them head on, the water explodes, and when they pass under the stern, the ship is lifted out of the water and the whole boat vibrates as the screws chew up the air.

And when it turns real bad there's no place to hide. The storms in the Atlantic can last up to three days. I sure was scared during my first storm. The waves were shooting over the foredeck, I was terrified of being swept away and lost to a watery grave; thankfully you had a line from the bridge down to the forecastle, to which you had to attach yourself before making your way along the deck.

I was taught how to steer the ship on that second voyage. I remember my first time and being scared that I would mess up. The officer who was up on the bridge with me on my first watch was very kind and understanding. He said, 'Now, Clifford, relax and keep it on the heading you are supposed to be steering. You are going to waver but don't react immediately, take your time and let it gently swing back and forth, that's the way a ship goes.'

He taught me that if you overreact then you are going to zigzag. He asked me if I missed home and I told him that I missed my mother. He said, 'You will find that you start drifting off when you start thinking of this and that; it's quite natural but try to pay attention to the compass.'

*

We had crossed the Atlantic and had been travelling up the St Lawrence River for two days and I didn't even know it. Its river mouth is enormous. It was a Sunday when we first began to see land. I could see little white churches dotting the land on either side of the river and their bells were ringing out.

When we finally got into Montreal it was quite an eye-opener. The immensity of it all, compared with my hometown, was stark. It had these tall impressive buildings; people dressed smartly in suit and tie. And on the docks the machinery was more up to date than back home. It was also the first time that I ever saw the Canadian Mounted Police. I sure liked their uniforms, and true to form I thought to myself, 'I would like to be one of them.'

*

By the time I joined my second ship, the *Masunda*, I was really comfortable at sea and looked forward to seeing more of the world. That wish came true when we took a load of anthracite coal to Canada and then went down the eastern seaboard of America and, lo and behold, there was Panama. It was the most beautiful country I had ever seen in my life, full of stunning lakes and fertile countryside. I could spend hours talking about the Panama Canal. It's a beautiful structure, right up there with the Seven Wonders of the World in my book. It's a mind-blowing feat of engineering. Before you go through you have to anchor at a place called Balboa Harbour and Panama City is on the other side. We anchored and went ashore.

Panama was very hot and humid with a lot of flies and mosquitos and soon after getting ashore we were thirsty so we headed into a bar. Inside were all these regular US Navy fellas sitting around. I sat at the bar and, being a sociable kind of guy, I said something to the Yank sat next to me, just to open a conversation.

'What ship are you off?' I asked.

He looked at me and said, 'The USS *Hardship*.'

I said to myself, 'Right, this sonofabitch wants a smack in the mouth.' Being a small fella never bothered me. I had learned to box back in my Boys' Club days. The guy wanted it and that was okay.

I said, 'What did you say?' He said, 'I damn well told you, the USS *Hardship*!'

So I said, 'You want a damn punch in the mouth, don't you, you sonofabitch?'

He said, 'Who's going to do that?' And he stood up

and he just kept rising; he was a giant with muscles for fun.

I said, 'I didn't mean anything.' And I walked off but the guy sat to my left, who was the carpenter from our ship, hit him a real wallop. There were fights going off all over the place, and, being so brave, I got down under a table.

These US Navy guys liked to mix it up but in those days there were no dirty fights, it was fisticuffs all the way. It was like back home on a Saturday night when all the boys would come down from the valley, have a fight, and afterwards everyone would be the best of friends; no hard feelings.

Later that night we settled in another bar where this solitary Yank was sat at a table. It wasn't a large place and he kind of sidled over and latched on to us. Now he had a loud mouth and when he heard our accents he started being disparaging towards the British and insulting to the Royal Family, while going on about how they had kicked our butts in the War of Independence.

Having just survived one brawl we tolerated him and I was surprised when some of the older guys started buying him drinks—he was already half cut. When he was totally wasted, almost unconscious in fact, the ship's carpenter said, 'Help me get this fella out of here.'

We slung an arm each over our shoulders and staggered him outside. I didn't know where we were going but the carpenter took the lead and we crossed the street where there was a small tattoo parlour. We went inside and slumped that Yank down on the chair and paid for the sonofabitch to have God Save the King tattooed on his chest.

*

In those days I was pretty much a loner; I didn't see the pleasure in sitting at a bar drinking all the time. I was the kind of guy who appreciated all cultures and here was my chance to see, for real, all those countries I had first heard of back in Swansea, sat at a wooden desk in St David's School. So whenever the opportunity arose I used to get on a bus or train and visit the villages on the outskirts of whatever port I had landed in. I used to try to talk to the people as best I could. It wasn't easy when there was a language barrier, but I would always try. I would sit down and have a coffee and get chatting in Pidgin English.

*

On another occasion we went up to Vancouver to pick up a shipload of timber to take Down Under for the Australian railroad. We were only in Vancouver, which was a beautiful place, for a couple of days before we got orders to go up river to an old Indian settlement called Esquimalt, on the tip of Vancouver Island.

That river was very fast and deep. We were capable of doing ten knots but, in real terms, we were only doing three or four going up that river (coming back down that river, with the current being so fast, the captain had us in reverse). When we got up there it opened up into a tremendous expanse of water, a big lagoon. I had never seen so many fish, jumping so high you would think that they were in the Olympics.

We were there for a week and it was one of the most pleasant experiences of my life; it felt like I belonged there. There were beautiful people who invited us into their homes and cooked us a meal. They said I should stay and work there, I really thought about it. Honestly, I could have lived and worked in that place, it was paradise, but there was no way I could turn my back on what was happening in the world.

*

September 3, 1939, sticks in the mind of all Brits as the Germans had invaded Poland. Distressed by the turn of events, Britain went on to issue an ultimatum telling Adolf Hitler to withdraw his troops. The whole nation had gathered around their wireless sets that September morning to hear the British Prime Minister, Neville Chamberlain, break the disturbing news that a state of war had been declared with Germany.

We were in Montreal at the time and I couldn't get

over it; we were at war. We had guessed something was afoot because back home they were issuing gas masks.

The captain got us all together and we were told that there was to be no smoking on deck and when we put a light on we had to make sure that the porthole was covered. We were also told not to use flashlights. He said that if we were hit with a torpedo, then we would know what he was talking about. If we showed a light we gave our position away, which wasn't easy to detect in the dark; that's all the conning tower of the submarines needed and you were sunk. We also had quite a few evacuation drills.

I had no experience of war. Growing up in Swansea I remember watching the veterans of the Great War gathering around the cenotaph, with their medals on their chests and heads bowed, on Armistice Day, but I knew very little of what it all meant. There was one incident involving Mr Berry, who ran the shoe repair firm where I worked for a while. I called at his home one time to see his sons and found him crying in the corner. I had asked him once if he had been in the war and he had said yes but he did not want to talk about it. I later learned that he had been hit by machine gun fire, all down his side, while serving in the trenches in France.

On this particular day he was standing in the corner, the poor man, crying and all agitated. Mrs Berry said, 'Don't pay much attention to him, Clifford; he thinks that he is going to die.'

That was my first real encounter with the devastation that war can bring. I was to get another, more sobering, indication of its carnage when we went down to Nova Scotia, where they were putting a convoy together.

We were in port when a British submarine pitched up next to us. I was working near the rail and when I looked over the side I saw, laid out on its foredeck, bodies that they had picked up out of the water, sailors from some unlucky ship that had met a U-boat. Later they had to take the bodies off the submarine and transfer them ashore for burial, but it was so cold they had frozen to the deck. It took some time to get them loose and removed to shore.

'This is bloody war,' I thought to myself. The realisation came to me when I saw those bodies. I will never forget that experience.

As we were sailing under the Red Ensign (the flag flown by British ships) we too were fair game so it was vital that we joined a convoy, and Nova Scotia was an activity of ships. It is a large province on Canada's North Atlantic coast, and was the ideal location for a staging post for the convoys before running the German gauntlet of crossing the pond. The ships would line up and the captains would go ashore to talk about strategic stuff and then they would come back and we would take off.

The convoys were essential to supplies getting back to Great Britain. Oil, gasoline, food, medicine, you name it, they were aboard these ships; I even saw one hold that was full of children's toys.

There was a lot of signalling with the lamp during the daytime. They couldn't use radio because it would be picked up by the Krauts. (We called the German's Krauts. It was part of the games of war. Hell knows what they called us.)

You kept in formation and you went as fast as the slowest ship; except when you came under attack—then you scattered. There's safety in numbers. If you were by yourself you were very susceptible to attack and you only had one gun. You had more firepower with a convoy, which didn't make things easy for the Germans.

We had a six-pounder gun fitted to our ship, right on the forecastle. When it went off it was so damn loud it shook the whole ship. It came with some navy boys, as the Merchant Navy guys couldn't handle that. There were six or seven of them on board in charge of that gun.

Besides the big cannon there were several machine guns on the deck. We used to practise aiming at barrels in the sea. I was quite prepared and ready should I be needed. We also had older, handheld rifles.

The Royal Navy ships also deployed depth charges to shake up the U-boats, or Hitler's Wolf Packs, as they were known.

You also battled the intense cold of the Atlantic; temperatures were so low men were sent up to the crow's nest to keep a look out for icebergs. I remember thinking, 'If we get torpedoed in this water, as cold as it is, then that's it, I'm gone.'

The convoy itself was a unique experience. In the early days we didn't get the navy escort in the mid-Atlantic. We used to get an escort going out, from the Canadian Navy, and on the other side, near Ireland, you would have British destroyers coming to meet you but, in the middle, we were on our own so there was always an Our Father and several Hail Marys to make sure there was a higher power looking after all of us.

We were much more susceptible to attack the closer we got to Britain; air strikes from the Luftwaffe using Stuka dive-bombers—the noise was terrifying. They also came at us with surface craft, these little boats with torpedoes on them. They were zigzagging in and out of the convoy. We came under fire several times but weren't torpedoed, thank God.

*

I travelled in several convoys but I will never forget the first attack crossing the Atlantic. On the second trip back from the States we had been out seven days when all hell broke loose. I was down in the engine room when I heard a huge racket going on. I ran up topside and to the right I could see fires and ships burning. The Germans weren't stupid and they knew that the oil tankers would be in the middle of the convoy; so the U-boats used to surface in the middle and then, naturally, there would be panic.

I thought, 'We are next.' But we escaped attack.

Many years later I discovered that my first ever ship, the *Selvistan*, was hit by a torpedo a few months after I had left the Merchant Navy and was sunk with the loss of five lives.

*

Despite it all, the esprit de corps of the men, the English, Irish, Welsh and Scots, could not be faulted. We were all together as a unit, appreciating each other, understanding that if things went wrong we would be there for each other. There was no bullshit about a guy being from a different country: we were all friends. The older men were especially on the lookout for the youngsters.

Most of us on board, being merchant seamen with a few years under our belts, realised the importance of our role in the war effort. The British Army, Royal Navy and Royal Air Force were doing their job and most men that I spoke to thought that it was only fair we did ours. Yes, we could get torpedoed or go down one way or another, but we didn't spend time thinking about it; that wasn't productive anyway. You just got on with what you had to do.

We didn't talk about it much; you just accepted the fact that you were in the British Merchant Navy carrying goods across the Atlantic for Great Britain. We needed it, we needed the gasoline, we needed the food, we needed the medical supplies and so on. We knew that we had a job to do. We signed up under our own free will—nobody forced us. It was the proper thing to do, who else was going to feed the nation?

I don't think enough credit has gone to the Merchant Navy, especially those who did the Archangel run in the Arctic Ocean. Weather-wise it was foul up there pretty much all the time. I wasn't on those runs, thank God. They saw lots of enemy action because they were going to Russia and had to pass the German navy bases in the Norwegian fjords; and if you got hit up there and went in the water, you only had about a minute to live. And from what I picked up, the Russians weren't too nice to you when you got to port anyway.

*

Thankfully, I wasn't in a lot of convoys, as I did a lot of sailing down in the Pacific and in African waters – but they, too, held dangers. I remember very vividly standing on my third ship, the *Kaituna*, at night and seeing the sky lighting up on the horizon, close to African waters. The captain informed us that it was activity from German battleships. I saw this not once but a number of times. To my knowledge there weren't any convoys in the Pacific and the German battleships acted as raiders, going after single ships which were just delivering their cargoes on regular Merchant Navy business.

Later, when the Japanese came into it on the side of the Nazis, they brought submarines in the Pacific but, thank God, I never encountered any because we had a damn good skipper who managed to avoid them. I also remember reading about a German pocket battleship called the Admiral Graf Spee. She had a top speed of twenty-eight knots and was responsible for sinking a lot of ships in the South Atlantic.

I thought to myself, 'What if we come into contact with that?'

Thankfully, she became a number one target for the Royal Navy and they finally caught up with her just off the South American coast.

There were several ships outside Buenos Aires waiting for her, including HMS *Exeter*, HMS *Ajax* and HMS *Cumberland*. Faced with certain defeat her captain, Hans Langsdorf, scuttled her at the mouth of the River Plate. When he did that he saved the lives of hundreds of young German sailors, because if he had gone out and taken on what was waiting for them they would have been blown out of the water. I admired that. The captain went down with his ship as I remember.

*

I spent the best part of a year south of the equator, including making a couple of trips taking cargo across the Tasman Sea between Australia and New Zealand.

On my last visit to Australia my life journey was to take another significant turn.

By the time our ship was in Freemantle, Perth, I was seventeen but could pass for eighteen, and, despite playing an important role in the war effort within the Merchant Marine, I wanted to do more. My plan was to get into the Royal Australian Air Force as a radio operator. I had learnt Morse code on board ship from the boys in the radio room and I could send and receive at a respectable speed. I wanted to use that skill to get closer to the action.

I left the *Kaituna* at Freetown. I had been out the night before and had met a girl who took me back to meet her folks. She lived quite a way out of town and when I overslept there was no way I was going to get back to the ship in time.

With the ship having sailed I ended up sleeping on the beach. I had my coat on my head and I covered myself in newspaper and heaped sand on top because the bugs would bite you pretty badly. When I woke up the next morning I saw several mounds on the beach around me and I thought, 'I've got company.'

When my new companions got up, and I said howdy, we started talking. None of us had any money so someone said, 'Let's go and see the Salvation Army.'

They were open at that time of morning and they invited us in and said we could have some coffee, doughnuts and sandwiches with the only proviso being we first joined in their service; so there I was beating a tambourine singing along to the hymns.

After an hour or so the Salvation Army director said, 'We are going to stop now and have some breakfast.'

Now we had been looking at that spread all the way through because we hadn't eaten.

After breakfast we went out into the grounds of the headquarters and the director said, 'You don't have to do any work but if you want to do some cleaning or chop some logs we would appreciate it.' Which we did. He then told us that if we wanted to stay for a while, we were more than welcome. Which we also did.

From that day, every Christmas when I pass a Salvation Army collection box, I always put a few bills in because they were a lifesaver.

*

There were four of us kicking our heels along the beach waiting for a ship. One of the guys was a deserter from the Australian Navy, another, a big African guy, had deserted from somewhere or other, and this third guy smelt like trouble if truth were told; he would put the bite on you for a smoke or whatever and so we called him Snakebite. He wasn't quite with it, but he was good with his fists.

Each day we would go down to the shipping office

but there wasn't too much work around until a Dutch ship called the *Sloterdijk* turned up; she was part of the Holland America Line. The Germans had invaded Holland so she couldn't go back to Europe.

I signed on with the plan of getting a ride to Sydney, where I would be able to enlist in the Royal Australian Air Force. The others, not wanting to enlist, saw the chance of a passage to Sydney and richer pickings too good to miss and joined me.

*

My plan looked to be taking shape, however, once we had set sail, I got to talking to one of the crew and he said, 'We're not going to Sydney.'

'Where the hell are we headed then?' I asked.

'Cape Town,' he said.

'You're kidding.' He wasn't. I told Snakebite.

'The sonofabitch,' he said, 'I'll see about this, I'm going to talk to the captain.'

The rest of us followed and once on the bridge we looked at the captain and we all said, 'We want to get off.'

He looked straight back at us and said, 'Under maritime law I could throw you all in jail right now. And you would stay there until we reach Cape Town.' He was right and we all thought on it some.

Then he said, 'You have a decision to make; either

45

you work your way and behave yourselves or you are in deep trouble.'

Suddenly Snakebite jumped forward and growled, 'Listen, I have a piece of rope here, I will hang you, you sonofabitch.'

Now the captain, who was a big guy, asked incredulously, 'What did you just say?'

'I said, I am going to hang you.'

'Oh no you're not,' came back the captain and some crew members grabbed hold of Snakebite and put him in the lockup. As they led him away the captain called, 'You will stay there until you become a good man.'

He turned to the rest of us and asked, 'Are you going to work?' We all said yes and went back to work.

*

My plan of getting closer to the action was put on hold for a while and I settled back into the routine of life aboard ship, which always had its lighter moments, even in wartime. To prove the point, a week or so later we pulled into Cape Town and dropped anchor. As we were unloading our cargo into barges a canoe paddled up. A huge black gentleman with some kind of tribal headgear on was peddling beads and trinkets; he also had a little monkey on board.

He stopped alongside and as we were leaning over the side to do some business with this chap, with a basket we had on a rope, the monkey suddenly made a break for it, climbed up the rope and got onto our ship.

The monkey was running all over the place, into the galley stealing food and then shooting up the mast and, I swear, he would pull faces at you. This went on for a couple of weeks. We couldn't catch him – he was very sensitive to people. Then one day he was sat on top of number one hatch and he was wearing a toupee on his head. The captain came running up and he looked different—it was his toupee. We never knew he wore one.

He shouted, 'Grab that damn monkey and put it in a cage; we're going to put him off wherever we land.'

That was the order of the day but the monkey didn't know anything about it. Eventually we had him cornered. Then, as one of the seamen approached with the cage, he jumped overboard into the water. There was no way of saving him. We didn't want to harm him but he got scared and jumped—with the captain's toupee still on his head.

*

We then spent time sailing along the African coast, visiting places like Cape Town and Sierra Leone, picking up cargo to take across to South America.

When, a little while later, I ended up in Buenos Aires I was surprised to see German navy boys, in uniform, walking around the town. I thought they were probably from the scuttled *Admiral Graf Spee*. Personally I thought that they should have been interned, but they seemed decent enough, there were no hard feelings. War is war.

*

When Pearl Harbor happened on December 7, 1941, and the United States finally entered the war, our cargo changed to transporting troops.

After sailing up to New York from South America, we berthed in Brooklyn while they rigged the ship out for troop transport. Our first job was to take a load of American GIs to Casablanca in North Africa. During that voyage I got talking to a young soldier on deck. He was barely a boy and was acting kind of strange, so I tried to be nice to him.

I said, 'What's going on?'

'I miss my Mom,' he replied.

'Oh,' I said. 'Where are you from?'

'Are you familiar with the Brooklyn Bridge?'

'Yep.'

'I live under the Brooklyn Bridge.' There was a housing development there.

He asked me, 'Where are we heading?'

'We're going to Africa,' I told him.

'Oh,' he said, 'I don't know if I'm up to it.'

'You're up to it sure enough,' I said. He fell quiet for a while and so I asked, 'What would make you happy?'

He said, 'If my Mom knew that I was on a ship heading to Africa. If you can do that for me I would be all right, I could handle it.'

When I returned to New York I had his address in my hand and I caught the subway and got off in Brooklyn. I found the apartment and knocked on the door. His mother opened up and I explained that I had a message from her son. She turned white but I hastily added that it wasn't bad news.

She invited me in and I explained how I had met her son on the ship and how it led to me being there.

'I can't tell you where he is,' I said, 'because of the special Secrets Act, but I can tell you that he is safe and in good spirits and that he said to tell you that he loves you.'

She started bawling and then poured me a cup of coffee and asked, 'Where is he?'

I repeated, 'I can't tell you but you would be proud of him; he's a good lad.'

'Was he down in the dumps?' she asked.

I said, 'No, he was all right but he misses you.'

*

Casablanca was a real eye-opener for a Swansea boy. I was only a little Welshman but someone told me about the

49

Kasbah, where you had all these dancing girls, the nightlife and the market, and I told myself I'm going to see that. I came across all these beautiful girls hanging out their windows saying 'Zig zig'. I didn't speak any Arabic but when they made a sign with their hands I realised that I had wandered into the red light zone. I kept on walking.

I came to the market and they were selling gold trinkets and I bought something small—as always, I didn't have much money—for a special girl I had met back in Manhattan.

I had bumped into a fella by the name of Joe Harris who was a Welsh speaker, originally from Bargoed in the valleys of south Wales. I had met him and his wife at a dance in New York organised by the St David's Society, which is made up of Welsh expatriates. They befriended me and I stayed with them for a while.

Now they had a daughter by the name of Vera, who was one sweet gal and I was rather keen on her, but once again my plans were to go belly up.

One evening I ended up with Joe in an Irish bar called The Shamrock. He liked his drink and I went along for the company. We sat at the bar and further along this guy was singing an Irish song while his wife sat next to him. Now for some reason he got to thinking that I was trying to make out with his wife. I wasn't.

Joe said, 'We have got to be careful here, that guy is drunk and he wants trouble.'

'Come on let's get out of here,' I replied.

But as we were walking out this guy grabbed me and pulled me in close. As he did I really smashed him, I wanted to hurt him. I had no designs on his wife; I was a good-looking fella and could get any girl I wanted.

Then his mates started to come in so Joe, who was a big guy who used to be a blacksmith, stepped in. We ended up in quite a fisticuff.

When we got back home, Mrs Harris looked at us and said, 'Oh my God. Look at the both of yous. He's got a black eye and you have a split lip.'

Then she looked directly at me and said, 'So you are taking my husband out there and fighting in the bars, are you?'

I said, 'No, Mam.' But she wouldn't hear it and said, 'Bugger off and don't come back here again.'

So that scuttled any hopes of Vera and me; broke my heart because I guess I loved her.

*

I had sailed into Manhattan a few times and I was beginning to find my way around, although you can imagine how my eyes near popped right out of my head on my first visit. It is such an impressive sight as you are coming into New York harbour; what catches you first is the Statue of Liberty and then, off to the right, Ellis Island. Then you see all the skyscrapers ahead of you and it stops you in your tracks. I was overwhelmed. The tallest building in Swansea was the Weaver's Flour Mill or the Orchard Street police station, with its clock tower—they would have been dwarfed by these monoliths.

I had an opportunity to go up to the top of the Empire State Building. You could go way up to the sky deck and go out and walk around; I could feel it swaying slightly back and forth, I thought we were going to have a crash.

And they were big people too, in fancy clothes; it was a long way from the old flat cap and loosely fitting jacket I was used to because you didn't see too many heavily weighted people in Swansea during the Great Depression.

Out on the street, people swarmed along the sidewalks; all that noise and bustle created a huge energy. The taxi cabs were in the thousands.

I don't know the exact moment that I fell in love with America but the more I saw of her the more I got to thinking about making the place my home. My dad had been right—it had everything and was the land of opportunity in every sense of the word.

One of those Eureka moments came after returning from a cross-Atlantic voyage on the Sloterdijk. We were berthed in Brooklyn and when I was through with my duties in the galley the chief cook said, 'Clifford, if you want to take off ashore that's all right.'

I got my trunks and went to a swimming pool that wasn't too far away. It was late evening and I only swam for a little while when all of a sudden this music started to play.

It was The Star-Spangled Banner: the American national anthem. I looked up and the American flag was coming down. What a beautiful sight it was. It was a big flag being lowered very slowly. I saw people touching their hearts and I followed suit.

When it was all over I asked one guy, 'Why did you touch your heart like that?'

He replied, 'It's for our country. To show some respect. You see, young man, this is the greatest democracy in the world.'

Being from St David's School in Swansea I didn't understand this word democracy so I asked, 'Democracy?'

He said, 'Yes, while you are in this country you have opportunity. It is the land of opportunity.'

'Tell me more,' I said.

He was a Jewish fella and he said, 'Here in this country you can become whatever you want to become.'

*

Before long it struck me that this must be a great country because of the way the people were dressed; they had a few bucks to spend, the food was ample and they were so nice. I thought, this is not a bad place to live—what I didn't know then was that within a year I would actually become an American citizen.

However, events back home helped hasten that process.

Swansea, being an important port and all, came to the attention of the Luftwaffe. After France fell, the town became in range of airborne attack and, slowly at first, the bombs began to rain down on the people and streets of my childhood, culminating in the near obliteration of the heart of little old Swansea over three devastating February nights in 1941.

In what became known as the Three Nights Blitz, from February 19 to 21, a total of 230 people were killed and more than 400 were injured. Amongst the dead— as I was led to believe—was my childhood pal Tom McCarthy; he was killed when a stray German bomb landed on the terrace house where he lived on a hill overlooking the town.

*

I was little more than a boy when I first sailed out of Swansea but after spending three years kicking around the world's oceans, you could say that my voyage into manhood was complete and I was ready to teach those Germans a few lessons.

Chapter 3

Basic Training

In late 1942 I took the big decision to say goodbye to my ship, the *Sloterdijk*, and found myself, at the age of nineteen, in a position to act on my father's advice. In the city where I had been so taken with the sight of the stars and stripes being lowered at the day's end in that swimming pool in Brooklyn, I had finally decided to jump in the deep end and try to make a new life for myself in the United States.

My immediate plan was still to join the armed services to fight. That was the most pressing matter. However, now that I was in America, it had obviously switched from wanting to join the Royal Australian Air Force (as a radio operator) to wanting to join the US Navy. The sooner I enlisted and got stuck in, the better, as far as I was concerned.

I had been back to Swansea from time to time, on the merchant ships—on each occasion I would take my brothers and sisters some presents and see them okay for a few bucks—and I kept in touch as best I could, without being a prolific letter writer, so I knew what was happening and it wasn't pretty.

Old Swansea was a fairly small town and the Germans ripped its heart out, both figuratively and literally.

If, following those harrowing February 1941 nights, I were to once more have taken that early morning stroll which took me aboard my first ship, it would have been mighty different. I would have been forced to cover my face to the acrid smoke and shy away from the flames, stumbling over piles of rubble, the dregs of bombed-out buildings blocking High Street, shaking my head in disbelief at the fancy Ben Evans store, where I used to love going as a kid, now an inferno-gutted shell. I would have had to detour around huge craters in the road left by high explosive bombs, pausing to say a silent prayer for the now roofless St Mary's Church, its shattered stained glass windows scattered like teardrops; I would have sidestepped ambulances, rushing down Wind Street to take the dead and dying to the General Hospital. Like the once magnificent ornate indoor market, from where I sometimes pinched food to survive, my beloved town was a twisted wreck.

I took it all personally, and don't forget the Germans had also taken a crack at us through the Luftwaffe and surface craft while I was in the convoys with the Merchant Navy; it was time for revenge.

*

Until you travel the world you never quite appreciate the reach of your country, and once again I was grateful to the Welsh men and women in the New York's St David's Society for making me feel welcome. Besides meeting Jo Harris and his family, I was lucky enough to get to know a paediatrician named Oscar Race, who invited me to stay at his home on Staten Island.

I had been to New York on a few occasions during my time in the Merchant Navy, berthing in Manhattan, either dropping off or picking up goods, so I had a basic idea of the layout of the city. Now, with time to kill, I set about exploring New York properly.

I would head down to lower Manhattan, around 42nd Street and Broadway, and a place called the Stage Door Canteen. A lot of servicemen and women used to hang out there and you would also see a considerable number of people from the entertainment business. It was a place to sit down, have a cup of coffee and talk while you were in Manhattan. I had my Merchant Navy pin on so people knew that I had been doing my bit.

After a couple of months of kicking my heels and not really making any progress with my navy plan, I was to find the answer right under my nose. After dinner one evening Oscar had asked me what I wanted to do with my life.

'I want to get into the Yankee Navy, if I can,' I said.

The next day he came back from his office and said, 'I can't get you into the navy but I can get you into the army.'

What I didn't know was that, besides being a doctor, he was on the local draft board.

And so, within ten days, I found myself standing on a platform in New York's Grand Central Station, early in the morning, waiting for a train to take me to the US Army.

I only had a little bag with me because they told me in a letter not to take any clothes, just to show up in what I was wearing and, once I had arrived in camp I would be fitted out.

It was only a short trip from New York City to Camp Upton, which was on Long Island, where we were issued uniforms and a toothbrush before being assigned barracks for the night. Camp Upton was a staging area where you only stay for a day or so, before being sent to different places in the United States for basic training. When the next morning came, all the others guys were shipped out but I was left behind. Nobody had called my name. The barracks were filled again with a new intake putting on American uniforms and within two days they too were gone but, once again, I was left on my own.

I was there for about ten days wondering what the heck was happening. I was walking around saluting everyone who moved until one day, while at the PX (Post Exchange—it was like a store on the base) I got to talking to an officer who had two bars on his shoulder which meant he was a captain.

I said, 'Excuse me, sir, I've been in this barracks for over a week and people are coming and going; I'm supposed to be going to camp to get some basic training.'

He said, 'After you have purchased what you want, meet me by the door.'

It was discovered that they had lost my army records. I was sent in to see a major and he told me not to worry about it and that they would ship me out in a couple of days. Two days later I found myself on a train heading to Fort Leonard Wood, Missouri, which was out in the Midwest in the untamed Ozark Mountains.

From Camp Upton, New York, up to Fort Leonard Wood, Missouri, was one long journey, and it's especially long when the train is overloaded with men, all new to the army, a lot of them missing their wives and their families.

There I was, just a little Welsh fella, surrounded by all these Yanks; Tennessee boys, boys with drawls from the Texas Panhandle, New Yorkers, guys from every state in the Union, or so it seemed. When they picked up on my Swansea accent they asked me where I was from and I said, 'Wales.'

'Where is that?' they asked. They had no idea; it made me feel a long way from home.

Eventually I fell asleep but I sure woke up in a hurry because my foot was burning. Somebody had given me a hot foot. It's where you take a match and wedge it between the sole and leather of an army boot, then light it. It was my introduction to army humour.

I jumped up and started dancing around trying to get my boot off which proved difficult because in those days you also wore gaiters laced all the way up your shin so it was pretty darn impossible to take your boots off in a hurry.

I was lucky they had only put one match in my boot and my foot wasn't burned too badly; but it still hurt. When I had calmed down some I noticed, sitting opposite me, were four guys from Brooklyn peeing themselves laughing.

I looked at them and thought, 'Right, you sonsofbitches.'

I sat there and waited until they fell asleep. Then I got out my own box of matches and put one in each of their boots. They were fast asleep, and the guy who had laughed most at me got two in his boot. I lit them all up and in a moment or two those guys just shot up to their feet and went ranting and raving all over the doggone place.

Eventually they came back to me and said, 'You did this, didn't you?'

'Yep,' I said. I couldn't care less. 'How does it feel?' I added.

'Bloody terrible,' they yelled.

'Yeah, that's the way I felt.' After that, they never disrespected me again and we got on well together.

We eventually arrived at Fort Leonard Wood at around one in the morning and pulled into a railroad siding. It was February and the snow was over a metre deep.

I had a duffle bag containing everything I had been issued: clothes, boots, underwear, all of it packed in tightly. We were also issued M1 Garand semiautomatic rifles with ammunition. Weighed down by all that kit we had to stand along this platform with it snowing heavy and bitterly cold.

We all stood in line, three deep, and this big guy came along who turned out to be our staff sergeant. He stood there and said, 'If any of you fellas want to mix it up with me, then now's your chance.'

He was chewing tobacco and would spit it out and then carry on in his southern drawl. I think he was from Alabama.

He then said, 'Y'all follow me now.'

We marched, with the snow and that wind and that freezing temperature, from the railway station to the camp three miles away. I'm not a big fella and I was struggling with my rifle and big duffle bag but, finally, we made it and were directed to our barracks. It was nice and warm and we were each assigned a bed on a bunk.

The sergeant got us all in a circle and said, 'You guys are going to be up at 0600 hours.'

That was bad news. It was already nearly 0400 hours.

Sure enough, just under two hours later he was walking up and down the bunks banging a garbage can lid with a stick shouting, 'Wakey, wakey, wakey.'

We were all in bad shape but we got up and stood

outside for roll call. It was still very cold and still snowing. When we got back inside we had to make our beds and then we had to fall in again before they marched us off to breakfast. I had never seen food like that in all my life. I'm talking pancakes, I'm talking pork chops, I'm talking steaks and bread. My eyes nearly popped right out of my head but I tell ya, we were hungry.

*

Basic training up in Fort Leonard Wood, Missouri, was to last for ninety days. The main purpose for everyone there was to get your body in shape, to get you mentally in shape and to prepare you for military involvement with the enemy. For example, they taught us to understand what an M1 rifle was all about, how to use a bayonet, how to charge, how to engage in combat, how to use hand to hand fighting, how to dig a proper foxhole. We used to have lectures on it all, even venereal disease.

We were taught the army's rules and regulations, about not going AWOL (Absent With Out Leave), and a whole load of other stuff. They gave you a taste of everything; I even spent some time in the kitchens.

*

The training was long, thorough and challenging. But then again we were young men—most of us were eighteen, nineteen or twenty-year-olds but there were some guys in their thirties—and by the time we came through it all we were in good condition.

They sent us on what they called forced marches in the foothills of the Ozark Mountains. Sometimes the march would be five miles and sometimes they would be ten miles, with a full pack. I don't recall the exact weight but I can tell you they were doggone heavy; if they weren't they would put in bricks to carry.

Some people did get injured from time to time, not many but a few, who had to go to the hospital. I remember on one particular occasion one guy was so bad he died because of the rigours of that march.

That's just the way the army was—they were training us for war and we had to be tough.

On other occasions we had to crawl under mesh wire while they would fire live ammunition over our heads. They also taught us how to throw hand grenades. You were talking live hand grenades. Keep in mind that once you pulled that pin out you only had six or seven seconds at the most, and sometimes it was a shorter fuse than that because the ladies making them didn't put the correct length in there.

When you threw a grenade you had to keep the timing in mind. You pulled the pin out with your teeth and you kept a grasp on the safety lever of the grenade—of course, when you threw it you had to let go of that lever and then it would detonate within seconds.

Later, when we were in combat with the Germans, there were times when you pulled that pin out and you would count to two before throwing it, the reason being it would go off right over the machine gun nest or whatever target you threw it at.

Most of the guys were baseball players; it was the national sport, so they really knew how to throw. They were accurate, which is more than I can say for myself.

*

After about a week or so I was sat in one of the orientation classes when a fella tapped me on the shoulder and said, 'Are you Guard?'

I said, 'Yes?'

'Come with me,' he replied, 'the captain wants to see you.'

We went in his office and there were a couple of FBI agents in black suits waiting for me.

I was standing to attention when the captain tells me to take a seat. Once I had sat down one of the agents said to me, 'Where are you from?'

'Swansea, south Wales,' I said.

'Where in Swansea?' I told him the name of the street.

He looked at his buddies; they knew all of this, they knew about my mother, my grandmother, about Swansea. They continued to ask me questions.

'Were you in the Merchant Navy?'

'Yes.'

'And you're now in the Yankee Army?'

One of the agents, a real educated fella, said, 'Now's your chance. Do you want to stay in the army or do you want us to send you back to Great Britain?'

I looked at those guys and said, 'I want to stay.'

They said, 'Are you sure now?'

I said, 'Yep.'

They got out a piece of paper, with all legal stuff on it, and gave me a pen; and I signed it. When I signed that piece of paper it said, in effect, that I wanted to stay in the United States and become an American citizen. It didn't make me an American there and then, it implied that I wanted to stay and become an American citizen.

I asked, 'Where's that piece of paper that tells everyone I'm an American?'

They told me I would have to wait until I was ordered down to the Federal Court to be sworn in.

*

After basic training I had orders to go down to Fort Indiantown Gap in Lebanon County, Pennsylvania, which was the staging area for what was to become my home in the United States Army, the 3rd Armored Division.

I had to stand in line to see an officer whose job it was to hand out assignments. When it came to my turn

65

the officer said that they wanted to put me in the kitchens.

'No way,' I said. 'Those German bastards bombed the living hell out of my hometown. I want to have a go at them.'

'Okay,' he said, 'we'll put you in the 23rd Armored Engineers.'

I didn't know what I was letting myself in for because that meant explosives; I became a combat engineer.

We weren't at Indiantown Gap for very long and our time was taken up with even more lectures, enforced marching and putting into practice what we had learnt up in Fort Leonard Wood. It was pretty much more of the same except that everything was now done with the emphasis 'By golly, now I am real army'.

Indiantown Gap gave me an opportunity to understand that I was *now* a soldier. I was also training alongside other 23rd Engineers. We were taught how to build makeshift bridges and it was hands-on with the equipment. For example, we were given the opportunity to fire .50 calibre machine guns. We also did a lot more training with explosives and defusing mines where there would be a fire cracker inside waiting to scare the living daylights out of you if you did something wrong.

*

I must have been making the right sort of impression because being from Wales, which they all confused with England, I had picked up the nickname Limey, which kind of stuck and I didn't mind. (The name itself dates back to the British sailors of old who turned to drinking lime juice to help stave off scurvy).

Then came one particular incident that really broke the ice and got me accepted as one of the guys. We were in the barracks one afternoon after doing a five-mile hike. We were tired and sitting around shooting the breeze, and the guys were kidding and having a go at me.

Then one of them said, 'Hey, Limey, who is that picture of on the wall up there?'

I can tell you I didn't study American history when I was sat in St David's School in Swansea. And I sure didn't know at that time that it was a picture of the first President of the United States, George Washington; his picture was up on the wall in pretty much every US barracks.

I took a moment and then I said, 'I know who that it is; it's Babe Ruth.'

They laughed and laughed and from that moment on I was accepted and had good friends. When I said that the first President of America was Babe Ruth, well known in the United States for being a famous baseball player, they thought that it was the funniest thing that they had heard in their lives.

It was while stationed at Indiantown Gap in Pennsylvania that I was assigned to another kind of posting—that of being part of the closest trio of buddies you could ever wish to meet.

Every soldier needs a band of brothers; it's the nature of the job. You team up in an attempt to keep alive. You cannot go through war without having someone to look out for you; and when you go through hell together you sure learn quick whom your friends are.

In my case it was myself, Ralph 'Trixie' Trinkley and Henry 'The Greek' Kallas. None of us were above five-and-a-half-foot tall—dwarfed by the six-foot-six giants from Texas who made up a large part of our division—and we were all less than 145 pounds. But we sure were a tough trio.

Trix was a coal miner from Pennsylvania, while The Greek was from Michigan but we never learned too much about him. He kept things pretty close to his chest, but he was girl crazy; with his black hair and Adonis features he could pull the broads, there's no doubt about that. He used to tell us about his campaigning with the women.

We looked out for one another; you couldn't have been any closer than me, Trix and The Greek. The three of us were always horsing around but if they needed help I was there and vice versa.

Now in the Babe Ruth episode, Trix and The Greek had laughed as loud as anyone but, looking back, the incident that really cemented our friendship occurred on our way home from the camp's PX one evening.

We were down there until quite late and on the way back to our barracks we passed the officers' quarters and what a sight we spied; on a window ledge there were around a half dozen or so apple pies cooling off in the late evening air.

Trix looked at me and I looked at The Greek and said, 'Those are apple pies.'

The Greek said, 'I'm hungry.'

'Well, what are we waiting for?' asked Trix.

So we each took a pie back to the barracks, where everybody was asleep. We quietly snook into the toilet block and boy, did we have a feast. The only problem being, we were as bushed as the rest of the platoon and we couldn't wait to hit the hay; so we ended up leaving the evidence, in the form of the pie tins, behind.

The next morning, the whole barracks woke up to the first sergeant shouting.

'Which one of you miserable sonsofbitches stole the apple pies from the officers' mess?' he demanded. Trix, The Greek and me acted all innocent.

'The officers are out by three apple pies. I'm going to find out who did it and boy, will you be in trouble,' he yelled.

Then he shouted, 'I'm going to inspect hands.'

We didn't mind because we had licked our hands clean; those pies were delicious.

'The whole platoon is grounded,' he snarled. 'There will be no leave to go into town for a week.'

We didn't mind because our bellies were full of apple pie. We talked about that incident for months, and it really bonded our friendship.

*

Come March of 1943 Camp Indiantown Gap was to see me go through one final initiation that was to shape the whole course of my life.

I was in the barracks and an officer came in and said, 'Limey, you have got to go down to the Federal Court in Lebanon.'

'What for?' I asked.

'You will find out when you get there but put your class A uniform on.'

So all dressed up like I was ready to parade before the President himself, I caught a jeep down there and joined a whole bunch of guys like me, some navy, some marines. I would say there were around twenty-five of us. We went into the courthouse and there was the judge sitting up on the bench. He started telling us about the United States, the Grand Canyon and the Rockies, in an articulate speech.

After he had finished his little commercial he said, 'I

just want to welcome you to the United States of America. I want you now, if you are happy with all this, to raise your right hand and say these words after me.'

It was, in fact, the allegiance to the United States of America.

Afterwards the judge said, 'That's it,' and we saluted and filed out.

Some may question how I could sign up for another country, but my conscience is clear on that. I had done my time with the British Merchant Navy doing the best I could in helping to bring food and other supplies back to Britain, so I felt very comfortable with my decision. I felt quite proud that they would allow me to become an American. I had written to my Mam with the news and she wished me all the luck in the world, adding that as long as I came back and visited once in a while it was nice to have a Yankee in the family.

As I was leaving that courthouse I saw the judge by the door and I said, 'Where is my certificate of American citizenship?'

'You are going to get that piece of paper soon enough but you sure ain't going to get it today,' he replied.

'Why not?' I asked.

He said, 'Because first, you have to serve your time as a soldier and get an honourable discharge from the United States Army.'

I just nodded and walked out into the bright sunshine of my newly adopted country. I didn't know at that point in time that I was to earn that citizenship—and the right to be as American as George Washington himself—many times over on the bloody battlefields of Europe.

Chapter 4

Off to England

In late August of 1943 we were told to pack our things and climb aboard a fleet of US Army two-and-a-half-tonne trucks. We travelled by convoy through the night and arrived in the early hours of the morning at Camp Kilmer, New Jersey. It was all very hush-hush.

Camp Kilmer was little more than a staging post for the US Army and, although the official orders had yet to come through, we knew that we were headed overseas—that was where the action was. Hitler had pretty much trampled all over Europe, and Great Britain stood more or less alone and was in real danger of capitulation; thankfully, the US Government had realised that that would not be a good thing.

Our short stay in Camp Kilmer was filled with lectures on what to expect 'when the time came' and we were shown battle indoctrination films aimed at preparing us for war but, in hindsight, nothing can prepare a man for what we went through. We were also given the usual injections and a final physical examination along the lines of, 'You're warm, you're in.'

After a few days we were then given a twelve-hour pass so we decided to make the most of having New York City on our doorstep. It was the first time that neither Trix or The Greek had been to the Big Apple so, for once, I called the shots.

We enjoyed ourselves in Manhattan with the lights and what have you, something nice to eat and the comradeship and meeting the people at the Stage Door Canteen. We weren't drinking heavy, to be honest, but we did enjoy the music and the dancing with all the broads there.

We hadn't been told when we were moving out; we weren't even allowed to tell anyone that we were in Camp Kilmer. You were trained by the army to keep your mouth shut and be careful whom you spoke to. Despite this, word must have leaked out, as a heck of a lot of wives or sweethearts found their way down to just outside that camp; there was an awful lot of cuddling up and a lot of emotion being expressed. Then the blackout order came—no one was allowed off the post proper and visitors were forbidden. We knew then that things were about to start moving.

On September 4, we boarded the two-and-a-half-tonne trucks again and were taken to Staten Island in New York. We waited in a long line, with our duffle bags full of kit and our helmets marked with our army numbers in chalk, to climb a gangplank onto the USS *John Errickson*. My army number is 32812865 and I will remember it until the day that I die.

Quite a few guys crowded the decks of that ship as she set sail on that mild September night. As we slipped away, we watched the Statue of Liberty fade from sight and there were more than a few thoughts on such a significant symbol of just why we were crossing the pond to put our lives on the line. Trix and The Greek were quite forlorn; it was slightly different for them compared to myself, because it was their turn to leave all that they had ever known behind.

We waited just off New York until around two dozen other ships joined us, including the USS *Shawnee* and USS *Capetown Castle*, which carried the rest of the 3rd Armored Division, and an escort of US destroyers and a battleship. Then, once again, I found myself in a convoy zigzagging across the Atlantic braving U-boats and the waiting Luftwaffe.

Once on board they had taken us below decks. She was a big ship and they had fitted her huge hold out with triple-deck bunks. There were a few thousand on that ship.

I turned to Trix and said: 'Come on, I'm not sleeping down here with all these guys and being seasick and everything. It's gonna smell real bad, real fast.'

We went up to the galley and I spoke to the chief cook. I explained about my background in the Merchant Navy and offered to work in the galley, doing any jobs the cook needed doing, whenever he needed them doing. The only stipulation I made was that I be allowed to sleep in a storeroom near the galley. Luckily he said he could use me and I managed to get Trix and The Greek in on it as well.

It was fantastic. We slept with the potatoes, onions, rice and canned goods instead of going down the hold. And with all that food around we were eating every other hour.

*

The voyage took about eleven days and was, thankfully, for the most part uneventful, although the land-lovers on board had a hell of a welcome to life at sea. During the first part of that route the offshore swells caused the ship to heave up and down, resulting in seasickness.

*

There was a lot of free time on board the ship because there wasn't any room to do pretty much anything. Back in the holds, bunks were shared, used in eight-hour shifts so you couldn't even sleep when you wanted to. We spent a lot of time talking about our families and telling stories about this or that. We played poker, there was a lot of reading, a lot of guys would just gather round and shoot the breeze, or walk around the ship. None of us really thought about what was ahead of us, we were enjoying the comradeship.

The only downside was the heads, or latrines, that stank and, in order to save fresh water, we had cold showers of seawater.

A few days out we were each handed a booklet entitled 'Behavior in Great Britain'—that confirmed what we all had guessed. You can imagine what it did to me being on that ship. I was coming home, so to speak. The guys used to kid me about that.

Quite a few of the guys were interested in asking me about England, although we had no idea which part we were headed to. I told them that the people would be very accommodating and friendly. I also explained that the beer wouldn't be cold like they liked it but that it would be warm.

'I'll drink it,' cried The Greek.

*

We arrived in the port of Liverpool, two days before my twentieth birthday, on September 15, 1943, and received a tremendous welcome from the British, despite the very visible scars of hardship.

I can remember coming down the gangplank and seeing all these British forces gals waiting to hand us sandwiches and cups of tea. Up above the odd Spitfire seemed to skim over the pods of large barrage balloons, which hung in the sky in an attempt to make it difficult for German raiders.

The young ladies made us feel very welcome, but what really struck me was how tired and threadbare the country looked. Great Britain had been at war for four long years, during which time the rationing, unrelenting air raids and loss of life, both at home and abroad, had severely tested the nation's spirit.

We had been told to be very sensitive to the fact that the British people had gone through a hell of a lot, such as the bombing and strafing of London and other towns and cities, prior to us guys showing up. It was good that we had that briefing because most of the guys, coming from all over the United States – you are talking from Texas up to Maine and across to California – didn't have a clue about wartime Britain.

*

After enjoying that welcome we climbed aboard a train to head to our new base on Salisbury Plain in the south of England. Towards the end of the journey we had to pull over and sit in a siding for a couple of hours because there was an air raid going on someplace. We didn't find out where, but it quickly focussed the mind.

When we got moving once more we went through a little town called Tisbury and got into a place called Fonthill Bishop in the early hours of the morning. It was chilly and raining a little as we unloaded our gear and settled into these big Nissen huts, which had been put on a large and picturesque estate, which was owned by the local Member of Parliament, John Morrison.

The whole area around Salisbury was taken up by the US 3rd Armored Division. You are talking about a lot of men, engineers, infantry, tankers, maintenance, administration and so on who were spread all over that area.

Most of the guys fell in love with the English countryside and quaint little villages with their thatched cottages, public houses with jovial wartime songs such as Roll Me Over, historic churches and other ancient buildings, but the US Army trucks sure put a dent in some due to all those narrow windy roads.

Now there are all sorts of big cultural differences between the United States and Merrie Olde England, and that was to be demonstrated soon after our arrival. Most of the guys I was with were from Texas and on that estate were these big beautiful horses, the Right Honourable Member of Parliament's pride and joy.

When they saw these horses they wanted a rodeo. The captain had to issue an order to stay away from the animals. The guys didn't pay any attention to that. The Yankee Army is like any other army in the world—we had respect for the officers but we had our own way too. And within a week they had a sort of rodeo going down there with all these doggone horses and villagers coming to see it.

Of course, his Lordship blew his top when he found out and all his horses moved on to some other place.

Some of the guys tried out a more English sport when they were challenged to a game of soccer by the nearest British camp; they were a parachute regiment, as I recall. Now it was hardly a fair contest as very few of the guys had ever played the game before, and we took quite a beating. Then the guys discovered rugby, and although they had no idea of the rules, those six-foot-plus 250-pound linebackers amongst us sure did enjoy smashing into tackles.

That time spent in Fonthill Bishop was a nice part of being in the army and we bonded ahead of D-Day. All the while training continued and intensified with road marches, obstacle courses, maintenance, all the familiar army drills. In the schoolroom we had lessons on aircraft recognition, camouflage, waterproofing and so on. We also did military exercises up on Salisbury Plain, building bridges, setting up machine gun nests and practising things the way they were going to be when we got to France, which meant that we slept out in our little two-man pup-tents. Each man had half a tent in his pack and you buddied up to get a whole tent just big enough for you both to get in out of the rain. I was with Trix.

*

All that tactical training was to come in useful when we planned a kind of unofficial covert operation of our own. Running right past that camp was a small river. Now some way or other we found out that on the other side of that water, way up a hill, there was a college for young ladies.

So Trix and The Greek said to me, 'Limey, how are we going to get across that river?'

There were notices on our side prohibiting army personnel from crossing but we didn't pay them any attention. I told the boys to take their clothes off and use our belts to tie them in a bundle on top of our heads. Then, naked, we climbed in the water. It came up to our chests and was cold as hell, but we got to the other side and had dry clothes to put on.

We made our way up that hill to see what was going on and, lo and behold, there were all these girls, in their late teens, screaming and laughing when they saw us approaching. Pretty soon many of the guys were crossing that river to see those girls. We would sit down and talk and laugh, there was no funny stuff going on, at least not that I saw.

In total we must have crossed that river three or four times. We thought we would be able to go dancing because they had a big hall up there but it didn't work out that way. Our captain got to hear about it after he received a visit from an angry headmistress of that ladies' college.

She said, 'I don't want to see any more GIs up at our college and if you don't stop it we are going to call the police.'

That sure put a dampener on things because the captain deployed a sentry to walk up and down that riverbank to make sure that the guys couldn't get across.

*

On the whole it was a very enjoyable stay and there were other forms of entertainment. Some of the local ladies in nearby Tisbury used to hold a dance for both the GIs and the Brits on Saturday nights. We got on with the British soldiers just great. They appreciated us being there; there were a few instances where some tough guys wanted to mix it up, but generally speaking it was a good time.

There was no drinking inside that dancehall. There would be American Military Police standing around making sure of that, but there were sandwiches and soft drinks. We used to dance to big band music, especially Glenn Miller in those days.

Sometimes you would have a date with a girl and go for a walk and sometimes the family would invite you into their home. The army had briefed us about this as well. We were told that if you were offered a cup of tea, be sure to accept it as it's a tradition with the British. We were also told that they often didn't have much in the way of food but it would always be on the table to share with you. Most of the guys that I knew were very kind and understanding. They would say, 'Don't take offence but here's something extra here.' Whenever we were going into somebody's home we would always bring something to contribute, potatoes, meat and, of course, candy for the kids. It was not showing disrespect to the people but was our way of saying 'We would like to help some'.

Sometimes the family would be overwhelmed. The guys were great with all the local kids; they used to come into the camp to ask, 'Have you got any gum, chum?' We gave them plenty along with whatever money we had on us.

*

We celebrated Christmas of 1943 together on the base. I couldn't get a pass long enough to go home and visit my folks and the rest of the guys, of course, were thousands of miles from home. We made the most of it and queued up for the telephone to place that special Christmas call—I never did because my Mam couldn't afford a phone.

But being the US Army one thing was for certain: the food was outstanding. The Greek was made up; he never used to chew his food, he used to inhale it. He used to catch me watching him sometimes and he would say, 'Limey, get your eyes someplace else; I'm enjoying my chow.'

*

I attended the Tisbury dance one Saturday night, only to run into a spot of trouble. I was more or less minding my own business while Trix was off at the bar and The Greek, no doubt, was chatting up the broads, when this gal came along and asked me to dance.

Now this big fella—by his accent he was from down south, maybe Georgia—took exception and came storming up and accused me of trying to steal his girl.

I said, 'When I'm through dancing I will see you outside, you sonofabitch.'

I was confident but I didn't know that he was packing a knife. I finished the dance and took off my uniform jacket and headed out the back. When I got out there he was laying on the ground. Word had somehow got to Trix that this guy from Georgia was planning on cutting me so about eight of my buddies had gone out and worked him over.

I walked up and said, 'Have you had enough, you sonofabitch? When you get up, you and me will go for it.'

'Limey, piss off,' he replied.

So I said, 'Are you all right?'

'Yeah,' he said wiping the blood from his lip, 'I've just been knocked around a bit.'

'Are you sure?' I asked again.

'Yeah, don't bother, I'm fine.'

'Come on then, I will buy you a drink,' I said.

He had learnt his lesson and I was not really one for holding grudges.

*

Most of the guys used their leave to do a spot of sightseeing further afield, with a lot of them venturing up to London, only to return with solemn tales of sheltering from air raids and seeing first-hand the destruction of large parts of the capital by the Luftwaffe.

The three of us went up to London on one occasion when we had weekend leave. We walked around a lot, seeing some of the sights. We didn't experience any bombing but we also saw the devastation. Trix couldn't get over it. Neither could The Greek. He said to me, 'These people have been through hell here. Limey, did you go through all of this?'

'Not really, I was away at sea but they bombed the hell out of my town, we lost a few hundred people.'

They were taking on board then what things could be like.

*

Talking of leave, there was only ever going to be one place I headed on my first forty-eight-hour pass; I left that camp and went back to Swansea, it was only six hours or so by train. I hadn't been back for quite some time, maybe two years. I had my big army coat on and I had two chickens, cigarettes, tea and candy like you wouldn't believe. Because the guys knew that I was going home they gave me all kinds of stuff.

I saw the cook and he said, 'Limey, when are you hitting Swansea? Come and see me because I've got some big greasy yellow stuff that's good for frying.'

When I left that camp I was like a bag lady. I got off the train at High Street station and my brothers and sister met me. I was in my uniform and Edwina said, 'You have to be careful in case someone thinks that you're impersonating a Yankee soldier.'

I told her not to be so soft. When we got home I gave my mother a hug and unloaded all that food, the tea and sugar; she was amazed.

We had a good talk about this and that before the rest of the family turned up in dribs and drabs. It was only a forty-eight-hour pass, so it was just one night and I had to go back, but it was one of the nicest moments that I remember with my family.

*

On the train you had a series of compartments in the carriages, which sat eight people, and a narrow corridor going along the side. The corridor was packed full of army and navy personnel. I was lucky to come across one compartment with six girls sitting inside.

I asked, 'Do you mind if I come in?'

'Not at all,' they replied.

After I had sat down one girl said to me, 'You look familiar?'

'Oh yeah?'

'Is your name Clifford?'

'Yes,' I said.

'Do you remember jumping on my back when you were a boy?' she asked.

'Are you Mona Cadogan?' I asked. She nodded.

Then another girl looked at me and said, 'You used to hang out with my brother and he used to make fun of you because you couldn't whistle with two hands in your mouth.'

I think her name was Thompson. Her brother and I used to mix it up from time to time but we became good friends.

I heard one of the girls say, 'Shall we give Clifford a bit of a drink?'

I thought to myself, 'What's going on here?'

Mona explained that they all worked together and were going on holiday. They managed to get their hands on a bottle of whisky, a couple of bottles of pop and some sandwiches. They gave me a drink and we got to talking about St David's School, the Boys' Club and that kind of thing.

They got off before Salisbury; I think that they were going down south to the beaches, Bournemouth or someplace. It was the most wonderful time, having a little drink and sandwiches and talking about our childhood with these young ladies. I never saw them again. I hope that they made it through the war okay.

*

Gas was rationed heavily, not that we had access to a vehicle in our spare time, but, like a lot of the guys, we had bicycles.

Trix, The Greek and me used to take off down to the village or go exploring the outlying areas. One time we ended up at this great big estate, with a large beautiful house, near Salisbury. We were walking around wondering what it would be like to be that rich you lived in a place like this.

Trix said, 'I'm thirsty, I'm going to knock on the door and ask for something to drink.'

A young lady answered the door, I think she was a maid, and Trix asked, 'Excuse me, M'am, can I get some water, please?'

She went to get some and when she came back his Lordship was with her.

'Hello, how are you?' he asked in a typical aristocratic voice.

Now keep in mind back in those days the class system was really quite strong in England, and this guy was the Lord of the Manor. We thought that we would be in trouble for trespassing or something.

'Would you like something a little stronger?'

'No thank you, Sir.'

He invited us into the hallway, which was enormous. Trix looked at me and I looked at The Greek. We all thought we had better get out of there. In all fairness, his Lordship was quite friendly and said, 'Would you like some tea?'

We said, 'Thank you, no. Water is just fine.'

'Where are you from?' he asked.

We told him that we were down there in Fonthill Bishop.

'I know the people down there,' he said.

We were very pleased with our brief visit with his Lordship on his estate.

*

Another time we came across this big manor house and saw a lot of men in the grounds. We went over for a chat and realised that it was being used as a hospital for injured servicemen. They were glad to see us. These guys, mostly British, had been wounded quite badly, probably back in Dunkirk or some place, a lot of them were missing arms or legs.

We gave them what cigarettes and candy we had on us; we went back there again with more cigarettes. It did make us think at that point that we didn't realise what we were getting into. We were enjoying the summer, we were enjoying Great Britain, we were enjoying the way of life. Our expectations didn't much go beyond that, but talking to these guys really alerted us to the fact that we were soldiers and this is what we were going to be exposed to.

And we wouldn't have long to wait either.

*

The order came through, right at the beginning of June, to move out of our billet and into our tents in the woods on the Fonthill Bishop estate, with all our gear packed ready to get on the two-and-a-half-tonne trucks when they showed up.

It was at this point that we were issued live ammunition and that we knew things were getting serious. Why else would they be issuing us hand grenades, composition C (plastic explosives), .30 calibre ammunition? We took all that with us into our tents the best we could.

Then we saw these British aeroplanes coming back from what appeared to be across the Channel with these lines hanging out where the paratroopers had dropped. The invasion had begun.

*

When we left that camp we sure did leave a lot of bicycles, just outside the main gates, for the children in the area. We wrote on envelopes, which we attached to the handlebars, saying, 'Please give me a good home.'

We would need far more than bicycles where we were going.

Chapter 5

Omaha Beach

The two-and-a-half-tonne trucks finally showed up and we climbed aboard and sat back for a journey of some fifty miles through the darkness of southern England at night.

Around two hours later we arrived on the coast, judging by the salt in the air and sound of waves in the distance, and climbed out into the grounds of an enormous house, which turned out to be a commandeered hotel.

The next morning, June 18, 1944, we were ready for whatever was coming up but we were told that we had the day free. We decided to go down into Weymouth, which was to be our port of disembarkation, and enjoy what would turn out to be our last proper R&R (Rest and Recuperation) for almost a year.

I had never seen anything like it. There were servicemen from Britain, America, France, Canada; it was like the United Nations. The whole place was crowded. After two years of planning the invasion had finally begun and hundreds of thousands of allied troops had decamped to the south coast of England to wait their turn to cross that short stretch of water, the English Channel, and engage the enemy.

We were walking down the main street when we heard Glenn Miller music drifting towards us from this huge dance hall. The Greek turned to me and said, 'Limey, we will go in there and have a look around.'

We went inside; it was an enormous place, underneath The Royal Hotel on the Esplanade. I had never seen a dance hall as big in my life and who was on stage? Glenn Miller and his orchestra. We thought that it was pretty swell of the guy to help see the boys off like that. We talked about it for days afterwards.

The Greek could really dance; the foxtrot, the quickstep, and even the jitterbug. He went straight out there and did some moves. I wasn't in the dancing mood so I just hung around with Trix. Now after a minute or so Trix, who had two left feet and couldn't dance to save his life, turned to me and said, 'I'm going to dance.'

'Don't be so soft,' I said, 'you can't even move your left foot.'

'Well, Limey,' he said, 'you're going to show me what to do.'

The place was crowded but we stood up and Trix said, 'Just tell me what I have to do.'

I said, 'You put your hand on the shoulder and the other on her waist. Just walk with her slowly and move your shoulders a little bit with the music. And maybe turn around a little bit.'

'I can do that,' he said.

'You'll bugger it up,' I said.

'No way!' Then he stopped and asked, 'How do I get a girl?'

I said, 'See those girls sitting down over there? You just walk up and ask one of them to dance.'

He went over and picked the biggest, heaviest girl you could imagine. She was a big lady. They found some room on the floor and Trix attempted some kind of mad waltz and then his hand slipped down a little further from her waist. Now she wasn't having any of that.

He must have ticked her off because all of a sudden she stopped and shouted, 'I don't want anything to do with you. You can't even dance.' She stormed away, and he sauntered back to The Greek, who had wandered back over, and me, shaking our heads by the bar.

'What do you think of that?' he said. 'My hand only slipped a little bit.'

'We know where your hand was,' I said. 'We saw you.'

'No, I don't go for the heavy jobs,' he said.

'Yes you do.' He took some leg pulling for that; it was good to blow off a bit of steam before things got serious.

*

That night we went back to our digs expecting to move out the next morning but we didn't. Instead we went into lockdown and couldn't go back into Weymouth;

94

that was off limits. We spent the next few days going through final preparations and waiting around like caged tigers until the morning finally came when we were woken and told that we were moving out.

We left that billet on foot at around four in the morning. It was raining, it was dark and it was bloody cold as I remember, and we made our way down into the harbour from where we were taken by tenders across to our ship, which was anchored out in the bay. After a while we left our mooring and moved out into the Channel to wait on the convoy; the British, American and the Canadian navies were there to escort us across to the Normandy coast.

The weather was still terrible; we didn't even know if we were going to be able to land once we got across. May had been a sweltering month but June turned out to be one of the wettest and most unsettled on record.

Our vessel, known as an LST (Landing Ship Tank), was enormous, around 100 metres long. You are looking at probably twelve or fourteen half-tracks (armoured personnel carriers with traditional front wheels that steer combined with caterpillar tracks at the back) and tanks lying in the bed of that thing. It had twin engines and rudders and reached a top speed of twelve knots but, because of its very design, it needed to land on the beach and had a flat bottom, which, with the sloppy seas, made it one hell of an uncomfortable ride.

We were issued with motion sickness capsules and

vomit bags but for most of the guys they were of little comfort.

We spent the majority of that voyage sat in our half-track in the hold. We were allowed out to go up to the galley for food, but you took it in turns. It wasn't that long a voyage but they fed us good; it was just a shame that Trix and The Greek threw it all up.

*

The code name for the actual invasion, which has gone into the history books as the Battle of Normandy, was Operation Overlord. The Germans owned western Europe and had built a string of defences, known as the Atlantic Wall, from Norway all the way down to Spain, but the allies targeted a fifty-mile stretch of the northern French coast for the invasion.

The landings themselves, or Operation Neptune, also became known as D-Day, and saw the largest amphibious invasion in history. At 6:30 a.m., on June 6, 1944, over 160,000 American, British, Canadian and other Allied soldiers hit those beaches with the help of five thousand ships supported by what seemed like every available Allied aeroplane able to fly; since midnight paratroopers had been bravely bailing out behind enemy lines.

The beaches were codenamed, from east to west along the coast, Sword, Juno, Gold, Omaha and Utah; again names that still resonate today but none more so than Omaha, which proved to be the most costly.

Omaha was taken by the US Army with the 29th Infantry Division, joined by the 1st Infantry Division and nine companies of US Army Rangers, having the honour of touching down first. For once the intelligence guys got it wrong and Omaha, at around six miles long, far from being a soft touch turned out to be the most heavily fortified beach of the lot, with high cliffs defended by well-placed bunkers and pillboxes along with mortars, machine guns and artillery.

The Navy had been shelling the beach for some time prior to the assault—unfortunately the shells and rockets fell way short of any German defences. Similarly, the bombs dropped by our planes completely missed their intended targets, mainly due to the cloud cover, leaving the well dug-in German defenders at full strength to oppose the incoming troops.

The guys were taken by complete surprise as they expected only minimal opposition. It soon became apparent that a major disaster was taking place. The invasion had been timed for low tide to avoid the worst of the sea defences but that meant a long trek up the exposed beach, which became nothing more than a slaughtering ground for the fearsome German machine guns. This was also carried out without heavy armour as the plan to float special tanks in to the beach failed miserably; these duplex drive tanks, or Donald Ducks as the guys called them, were Shermans with a canvas screen that was supposed to allow it to float but they were released too far out and waves of up to six foot sank them to the bottom.

Omaha Beach was won with the blood of around two thousand of the bravest of the brave All American Heroes who deserve our endless respect and eternal gratitude.

*

Being part of the 3rd Armored Division, Trix, The Greek and I were somewhat fortunate in that we had to wait until the beach was fairly secure, because of the difficulty of getting all those heavy tanks and half-tracks off the ships and across the sand, and so we were spared the hell of those first few days. In fact the French later gave a gold-plated medal to all Allied soldiers who were on that beach during the month of June but no later.

When you see war movies like *Saving Private Ryan*, *Band of Brothers* and others, they give a fair portrayal of the vicious battle conditions that frontline soldiers were involved with, almost on a daily basis, throughout the major campaigns in the European theatre of operations in 1944-1945. In all honesty it did not ease up much. When we got to the land on top of that beach, we expected things to get somewhat easier, but they did not. That's not playing down what those first-wave guys went through—they got killed in their hundreds getting off their craft. It was a real bloody introduction to heavy combat.

*

When we dropped anchor off Omaha it took a while before we could finally get ashore because of the weather; huge storms out in the Channel delayed the landing for days. We spent the time keeping occupied as best we could, checking and rechecking our equipment. I'm sure a lot of the guys looked around and wondered how many of us would make it back.

We weren't allowed up on deck that often but, from the times I was able to go up, I will never forget the powerfully intimidating sight of the invasion armada—it was huge. The sea was more ships than water. Barrage balloons had been floated above and British and American fighter planes were overhead at all times engaging in active combat to provide cover for us troops and equipment.

It was also during that wait that I took the opportunity to volunteer to man the half-track's .50 calibre machine gun. It meant that I would be up there in the turret, with my head sticking out and exposed to enemy fire while the others remained inside the belly of the vehicle. Trix just shook his head at me and said, 'Do you know what the hell you are getting yourself into, Limey?'

'Don't worry about it,' I told him. I knew where I wanted to be. I didn't mind, it meant I would get a better shot at the Germans; it also meant that I was issued with a Colt .45 because there was no room up there to swing my M1 rifle in an emergency.

*

Then the order came and we went full-throttle for the beach; it was June 23, 1944, a day I will never forget. The LST hit and its huge bows opened up and we began to roll. We hit a section of the sand called Point Charlie, where the beach master and his helpers brought us on.

We had only been told that we were heading for France. They didn't say Omaha Beach; of course we didn't know then what Omaha Beach was going to turn out to be anyway. It was a graveyard of broken equipment, smashed tanks and twisted landing craft, stranded in the waves. When I looked across all I could see were craters and explosions. There were still broken bodies lying around.

The fighting had died down a little and it was somewhat more stable when we went in but, even so, we were still within range of the German artillery and a lot of stuff was coming into the beach, with shells bursting in the air and, now and then, what was left of the Luftwaffe showed their faces. It was lively.

The British, Canadians and other forces were on our left-hand side. The only ones to our right, as you were looking inland, were the US 3rd Army led by General Patton; once off the beaches he was to veer to the right and liberate that part of France. Our orders were to go straight ahead.

Soon after landing we had to get out of the half-track because it was spluttering and moving slowly, not a good thing in those conditions. The lieutenant got us all together and we headed up the beach on foot with the half-track slowly following us. They had cleared a path through the mines with the help of a specially adapted tank called a Mine Flail; out front it had a rotating cylinder with a number of heavy chains attached that deliberately set the mines off. As long as we stuck to that corridor we were okay.

I remember looking back and seeing all these carriers with their big doors waiting to unload the tanks that would hopefully thunder all the way to Berlin, but, right then, it seemed a hell of a long way off.

The beach itself was full of personnel, infantry, engineers; different skills were landing to do some work. We didn't have too much time to look around, as they needed the engineers to deal with mines and other obstacles up ahead.

As we got higher up the beach we saw a lot of wounded being attended to by various medical units, and they had squads going around collecting the guys who had got killed, giving them a proper place to rest before it was decided where they were going to be buried.

The path leading off the beach, up a steep bluff, had been heavily defended by two pillboxes, one on top of the climb and another one near the bottom, almost on the sand itself; they had taken a lot of our guys out before being destroyed. It had been a real bloody mess, for which the Germans were to pay heavily.

The first Germans I saw were prisoners being brought down that bloody hill onto the beach. They looked a ragged bunch of guys. They were put in a wire enclosure on the sand to wait until they could be escorted out to a ship and taken back to England—there would be no more killing for them.

My first encounter with the enemy for real came on the top of the beach. Trix was to my left and The Greek to my right, and we ran up and saw the infantry guys, who were in one hell of a mess because the Germans were trying to counter. There was lots of small arms fire but we stopped them; a lot of young Germans got killed, as well as American boys.

We could only move so far and then we were stopped. Although the guys had taken quite a bit of land on top of the beach, into the hedgerows, it was still a very nasty situation because we couldn't move. We had no place to go. The Germans were really holding hard to their positions.

*

Later on we were shown into a big field, just off the beach to the right, where we re-joined our half-track. We had to take some time to get the tanks and half-tracks ready for land work after coming off the LSTs. They had been prepared for water; for example, the exhaust pipe was extended and diverted to reach above the roof so water didn't get in and the engine had to be watertight. All that had to be reversed as quickly as possible after getting ashore.

While we were working there was still considerable small arms and machine gun fire going on but then we had a mighty scare, which we later learnt to laugh about.

It was late evening, the moon was out but it wasn't very bright, and someone shouted, 'Gas! Gas! Gas!'

We thought we were being gassed. I ran for my gasmask but Trix had it on. He had used his own for spitting out his chewing tobacco while inside the half-track so he had grabbed mine instead.

'Give me my gas mask,' I shouted.

'Take that one,' he said pointing to his own.

'You sonofabitch,' I replied.

Then we discovered that it was only the gasoline truck going around making sure all the vehicles had enough fuel before going into combat. Although we never knew at the time, that was just one example of the close camaraderie that would help see The Greek, Trix and me through the war in one piece.

*

We spent our first night in France in that field sat inside our half-track while all around us the fire and action went on into the dawn; it was pretty nasty but it was to become our existence for longer than any of us could imagine at the time.

Chapter 6

Hedgerow Fighting

At first light, with hardly any sleep, we followed orders and fired up the half-track and attempted to move forward. There were lots of our armour and infantry up there already but they were stopped just off the beach, near a little town called Isigny, because of the intensity of the German small arms and artillery fire; it was horrific.

In Normandy, hedgerows separate all the fields; it's known as Bocage country. It was a real mixture of woodland, pasture, rivers and streams, characterised by small fields that were divided by high hedgerows with thick bushes and trees, large and small, their base made up of solid banks of soil and stone, all served by a network of narrow sunken lanes. It was a system of farming that had existed since medieval times, and, at that time of year, bang in the middle of summer, with all those bushes and trees thick with green leaves, it was a kind of jungle warfare.

The Germans made excellent use of it. Visibility was almost nil at times and the high hedges and dense cover were ideal for ambushes and perfect camouflage for the Germans, who had had plenty of time to dig in and conceal themselves, all of which made attack a living nightmare. Snipers were everywhere and they had plenty of field guns and used them relentlessly; the fire was unbelievable and very accurate. They had zeroed— targeted—all crossroads and approach roads in the zone, something that I saw to devastating effect soon after hitting that beach.

It was the first time someone I knew got killed. He was a motorcycle dispatch rider. We didn't have great communications like you do today; there was a system of radio telephones, where they were strapped to a guy's back, but they didn't always work, as in this case. The messenger was called forward and I saw him being handed an envelope, which he placed inside his tunic, before heading off to the Command Post. But as soon as he reached a bend in the road he was blown to pieces; he ran straight into the fire of a German tank. They blew the hell out of him and I saw it. It tore me up; he was my old knife-packing Georgian pal from the dance back in Tisbury. In spite of our differences, though, he was still one of our own.

That was just one prime example of the hell of trying to establish effective communications in the Bocage, which at times led to uncoordinated chaos. We were just not prepared for that kind of warfare. Our armour wasn't suited to the terrain and found it hard to manoeuvre, while the battle-hardened German Panzer and Tiger tanks proved right at home in their defensive roles. If a Sherman tank tried to roll over a hedgerow it would expose its vulnerable belly and make a soft target for the German anti-tank guns.

With our half-track pretty much ineffective, Trix, The Greek and me, along with the rest of the squad, had no choice but to grab our M1 rifles and fight alongside the 36th Armored Infantry.

We were in the 3rd Armored Division and had been trained as combat engineers. Our job was to facilitate the forward movement of our troops by building bridges, clearing minefields, blowing up German armaments. But when there were no bridges to build or mines and explosives to deal with, we acted as infantry. Now that is a distinction that has to be made. Whether you were a cook, an engineer, or infantry, you were on the line, that's the way it was because it was so bad. We were right smack into combat; you worked with the infantry and you took the risks with the infantry. We were exchanging all kinds of fire back and forth trying to move from one field to the next, taking out as many of their guys as we could in the process.

One of our first engineering jobs, besides clearing mines, was to try to blast our way through those hedgerows. Initially we had to use explosives to get the job done. You would dig under the hedgerow, put in your charge, back off and it would blow the whole bloody thing. It would give you a passage to go through, you could run and branch off, but they were waiting for you.

Sometimes we used TNT but more often than not we used a Bangalore torpedo, which proved far more effective. The Bangalore torpedo was a metal tube packed with explosives that you could lengthen by joining two or more together. We would get one up to eight or ten-foot long and then manoeuvre it into the hedgerow. Then you lit a fuse at one end and ran like hell before it blew a gap big enough to get a tank through. It was also used to take out pillboxes and clear minefields.

The only problem with using explosives of any kind was that the noise and smoke of the explosion alerted the Germans to our position. But we were quick learners and after a few weeks we managed to adapt.

A real breakthrough, in both senses of the word, came about when some of the ordnance guys came up with a brilliant idea; they attached a bulldozer blade to the front of a tank to create what we called a hedge-cutter. It was fairly quick, clean and relatively quiet and made things a hell of a lot easier. There was also the rhino, where they made use of the German sea defences on the beach and cut a couple of lengths of angle iron and welded them to the front of the tank like tusks; when they drove into the bank they stopped the tank from riding up and enabled the guys to drive right on through.

I remember hurting or killing quite a few Germans who crossed my sight in those hedgerows. It was a terrible feeling taking these guys out and you had to learn to get use to the idea that this was war. But that idea didn't come quickly, it took a while to get used to the fact that it was a real-life situation; it was all totally new to us.

It must be said that the American Army was different to most other armies in as much as we were citizen soldiers; we were not regulars in any sense of the word. We came from all walks of life in the United States, all different occupations and professions; teachers, lawyers, common labourers, you name it. My company commander was an accountant. We weren't trained soldiers; we just had ninety days up in Fort Leonard Wood, Missouri, to get in shape. It was a case of one day you were working in a factory and the next you were being drafted into the US Army.

Keep in mind the Germans were well-trained, they had been at war for a long time, seeing action in Czechoslovakia, Poland, Holland, Belgium and, of course, France, before we turned up. They knew what they were doing. They were masters at it. The American forces, on the other hand, were green; we didn't know really what was happening.

*

That hedgerow fighting went on for weeks. Sometimes you didn't get any sleep at all, you could be on the go for a day and a half, sometimes two days or more, and you had to be awake because the Germans weren't sleeping, they were adding fuel – but we were taking it and giving it back in some measure.

People ask if you were terrified going into battle. I was more angry than anything else and it was the anger that kept me going, especially when they took out any of our boys. And they didn't always fight fair. One of their dirty tricks was to wave the white flag to lure the boys out. They would walk forward with their hands up in the air and then they would hit the deck to reveal a bloody machine gun behind them. I saw this happen on a couple of occasions. Once, I was in position behind a hedgerow and the infantry were there, Trix was to my right and The Greek to his right. We were okay but the infantry to our left took some casualties. It really drove us on.

Initially, it was a case of being careful, moving forward ever so slowly, being over-cautious and then, after a while, when things got nasty, you threw that to the wind and you really got tucked in and started to exchange fire in a very brutal kind of way.

*

There was danger everywhere but, being engineers, we also had to deal with explosives. How we did that under those extreme conditions I don't rightly know but it sure took a lot of guts. After a while you got used to not worrying about your own safety, because if you did, you wouldn't get the job done. Your own personal safety didn't come into it. We used to think: I'm not going to get it, it will be one of the other guys that gets it. A lot of guys thought that way but far too many of them turned out to be mistaken.

One thing that did scare the crap out of me, however, was seeing a German tank coming at me for the first time because I didn't have the experience of dealing with it. None of us did, but we learnt rather quickly to call on our training and use it effectively.

Up in Fort Leonard Wood we learnt that in the event of tank warfare you could turn to your trusty M1 rifle and you could put a mini rocket on it and you could shoot the tank; it was a wonderful piece of equipment.

You could hear those tanks coming before you saw them and we were ready for them with the rockets. Sometimes you wouldn't have a chance to use the rocket but you could run up and lob a hand grenade into the cogs; I did that on a number of occasions. It was either that or the tank would run over you. All I remember was the determination to take that damn tank out.

We saw a combination of German tanks and artillery carriers, what we called rouge guns, and boy did they know how to use them, particularly their 88mm cannon, which was a superb piece of gunnery. They would let them go throughout the day and night, shooting at this and shooting at that, with devastating effect.

When we first hit the beach and saw some of the

German tanks that had been blown to hell we noticed that 88 and we laughed at it, but very shortly after we learned to respect that gun. We thought them most peculiar and cumbersome in their length. Our guns, and the British guns, were much shorter and we thought that we had the right kind of approach but it turned out that those 88s were deadly accurate and they did damage, there was no doubt about that; they would rip through a bloody tank.

It was used by the Germans for anti-aircraft, artillery, on the tanks and sometimes on roadblocks – as you came around the corner; boom! That gun was the German answer to a lot of situations in combat.

*

When it came to sleep there was no predictability; you got it wherever and whenever you could and, although it was somewhat quieter at night, we had to be very careful because the Germans used to move at night.

We were young, we were fit, and we could go a couple of days without sleep but it takes its toll and if there was a lull in the activity, and there were lulls, you would either put your head down in the half-track, a foxhole or wherever the hell you were. You slept with all your gear on, including your helmet.

Whenever the opportunity arose to get some shuteye somebody had to stand guard. That person had to be aware and switched on because if they fell asleep it was a court martial offence and they could be shot because they had jeopardised everybody. This I almost found out for myself. At one point I was on guard duty, leaning against a hedgerow. I had been awake for maybe two days when I just dozed off. It was Trix who saddled up to me and said, 'Limey, are you asleep?'

I awoke with a start and said, 'No, I'm not.' He had scared me, but I guess he had saved my life and, perhaps, those of the whole squad. I never allowed myself to fall asleep again—I had learned my lesson.

*

We had moved into July and we were moving forward but not very rapidly. Sometimes it would take a whole day just to advance to the next field. It was a chance situation, moving the way we did. Sometimes you wouldn't be able to get the tanks in there so it would be a case of exchanging fire, getting over the hedgerow as best you could, and creeping forward on your belly. It was very, very dangerous trying to cross an open field. The Germans had little periscopes that they used to spot you; I don't remember us using them.

We would take a hedge and field and they would put on small arms and mortar fire and try to push us back. Most of the time when you took the field you held on to it, but sometimes you would lose it again; they would come in with so much fire you would have to back up, there's no doubt about that.

Yes, it was dangerous when you were moving from one hedgerow to another but move you had to. A lot of men were getting wounded or killed. I saw plenty of guys getting hit but you didn't have time to react, or help really, it would just slow things up. We had to rely on the medics, who would take care of them—that's just the way it was.

In the heat of battle I had a pocket full of little pebbles from Omaha Beach. Trix and The Greek had some too, and we used to throw them at each other if we wanted attention when there was a hell of a lot going on. When you are in that kind of situation you have to be sure that your faculties are telling you the right thing, otherwise you are going to lose your head. You get so absorbed at times you are off some place, so you get your buddy's attention by throwing a pebble. I used to tell Trix I would throw a brick at him if he didn't pay attention.

Naturally both sides kept their heads down but you would see the Germans popping up, once in a while, taking a chance. One of the old tricks that we used to use was Trix would put a helmet on the end of his rifle and hold it up and they would shoot the hell out of it; it would be full of holes. While they were busy aiming at the helmet The Greek and I would be further along and we would get a sighting and let them have it; and if they didn't open fire that would be a chance for us to have a look to see what was going on. After a while the Germans got wise to it and didn't fire knowing that we would pop up thinking it was safe.

It was a totally new experience for us. We couldn't move, we couldn't get our heads up to see what was going on without getting them shot off. Trix was 'volunteered' once to help recon the situation and find out what was in front of us. After crawling to a hedgerow on the far edge of the field with two officers, a lieutenant and a sergeant, they paused. On not hearing anything the two officers stood to look over the hedgerow and the sergeant was hit between the eyes. Trix saw him fall backwards and then the lieutenant was hit in the chest; both were dead. Being a damn good soldier Trix lay low and waited. He bided his time before crawling partially through that hedgerow until he could get a look at the strength of those Germans. He then waited until it was dark and made his way back. We had given the sonofabitch up for dead and were sure relieved to see him.

When we had the tanks on board it was a godsend because you could hide behind a tank as it was moving forward but, of course, the Germans had their anti-tank rockets that they would fire at the tank; there was all kinds of things going on.

When you were taking those fields it was very risky, they were well protected by the Germans and it was a very slow, dangerous and tedious kind of activity. You just tried to take a field at a time.

I remember the guys discussing whether we would ever break through and how we were going to do it because every time we made the attempt it was like a door closing in your face. The joke going around was we would be spending Christmas in the next field and it was only July. Personally I didn't give much thought to how long we would be there; you didn't have any time to think like that.

As for the weather, it was a typical European summer with some sun followed by heavy showers, and the nights were cold. But the weather was the least of our problems, as was sleep. Staying alive was our major concern, and making sure that we backed up our fellow engineers and infantry.

*

I remember one particular incident when I was fighting in the hedgerows. The Greek was on one side and Trix on the other, when I got hit by a piece of shrapnel on my knee. It wasn't very deep but it did bleed quite a bit. We carried bandages for instances like this so I just bandaged it up.

Then the guy on the other side of Trix bought it, he got killed. Trix looked up and saw these three Germans on a machine gun and he hollered something like, 'Machine gun on the right. About three hundred yards.'

Boy, did we lay in the firepower, making them lay

down. I don't know if we killed them or not but we certainly wounded them.

*

Although we had spent months and months training for it, back in Indiantown Gap, Pennsylvania, and Fort Leonard Wood, Missouri, only one time, thank God, did I hear the words, 'Fix bayonets.' It went along the line and when I heard that order I said to myself, 'This is the end.'

It was around 11 or 12 o'clock at night somewhere in the hedgerows. I remember leaning against the hedge, getting my bayonet out and slapping it on the M1.

It was a terrible experience to realise that you were about to go hand-to-hand.

I looked at Trix and he looked at me and said, 'What's going on, Limey?'

'I don't know,' I said, 'we had better fix these bayonets. Hell, this is World War One stuff.'

It was terrifying to realise what we were about to do. A lot of us had seen pictures of World War One. I know that I had the feeling that it was just like that, waiting for the whistle and going over the top knowing that it might be the end for you.

I have a lot of empathy for those men going over the top knowing that they would meet a hail of bullets; and not only that, we didn't have the barbwire set-up that World War One had.

We waited and we waited and we were listening; it was dead quiet. And nothing happened. Then orders came down to detach bayonets. It was one experience I never wanted to go through again.

*

Like any agricultural area there were a few settlements, small towns and villages, like Villiers-Fossard and Saint-Lô, which drew us out of the hedgerows and into some pretty nasty fighting. The town of Saint-Lô was to the west of the landing zones and along with Caen, which was targeted by the British and Canadians, it was one of the main crossroad towns into Normandy through which all major roads led, so, as you can imagine, the Germans were not going to give it up lightly.

We realised this when we saw that they had sent their 3rd Parachute Division in to defend it; they were the elite infantry units of the German Army—right there and then we knew that things were really going to start heating up.

As we were approaching Saint-Lô the intensity of the German response to us being there was considerable and terrifying. Saint-Lô took us to a whole new level of warfare; it was brutal. It was an on-going combat situation. It was a real opportunity for the American forces to move ahead and get away from the hedgerows and get into some really serious combat with the

Germans. We had the materials, we had the men and we had the guts for the fight. All the instruments of war were being used in terms of tanks, infantry, mortar fire, shelling, small arms fire and machine gun fire.

We blew up one hell of a lot of buildings to get through, something like ninety per cent of the town was destroyed. As one of the GIs later said, 'We sure liberated the hell out of this place.'

The only way to describe Saint-Lô is a bloodbath. The intensity of combat was unbelievable considering it was our first major battle. A lot of people got killed in and around that town. I was riding in the half-track but my job was up in the turret with my .50 calibre machine gun, the rest of the guys were down below, protected by the armoured plating. I was up there and my job was to make sure that I took out as many of the enemy as I could. I saw a lot of things going on that needed firepower, so I directed the .50 into that situation; and that's where, I believe, I killed a lot of guys. It wasn't an individual thing—it was just a mass operation that was going on. It was kill or be killed; it was war.

We nearly lost Trix in Saint-Lô. He was in a bind and we had to go in and help him out. It was some houses that were being taken and defended. It was a bloody mess. He was right in a situation where the Germans had him pinned down with small arms and machine gun fire. The Greek, who was to my right, hollered, 'Trix is in trouble.'

I looked over and saw Trix crouched down behind what was left of a piece of front garden wall or something. He couldn't show his head or they would have blown the bloody thing off.

Trix was shouting, 'Greek, Limey! Help!'

The Greek shouted at me, 'Get in there with the machine gun.'

We had Thompson machine guns at that time and The Greek moved in to his right while I edged closer on the left, and we really let go before switching to hand grenades; that's how close we were, we were talking hand grenades. We crept forward and were able to give Trix the opportunity to sprint back to us because we had their heads down, we were really pouring in the ammunition.

Keep in mind that there was firing going on all around; this was just a very small section of what was going on across the length of the line. When Trix came over he was all right but he was pretty shaken up because he hadn't been able to move; if he had, he would have been killed. That was a close call for all of us.

*

After taking Saint-Lô we were back into hedgerow fighting and back to square one almost. During that first month in Normandy there was a lot of activity but we were really hitting a brick wall in my estimation because the Germans were so well entrenched and used to combat. Part of the problem was the nature of the hedgerows that kept us pretty much pinned down, along with our relative inexperience. We did move forward from time to time but with the loss of a lot of guys.

Between landing on June 23 and up to late July, the 3rd Armored Division is said to have seen over eight hundred men injured or killed along with the loss of around a hundred and fifty tanks and other vehicles. The Germans were holding their line; they couldn't push us back and we couldn't push forward. It was an impasse. We had to do something about it or we would have lost our position. Things were so bad that a rumour started going around that they were going to take us back to the beach and away.

Then we were ordered to put down these highly reflective orange markers. They were around three yards long and perhaps a yard across. It must have been around 8 o'clock in the morning. We put stones on top to keep them in place and we did this all along the front line. I didn't know what the hell we were doing but they were very pretty.

We were then all told to pull back, almost to the beach itself, and it turned out we had marked out a bombing corridor, of some four miles by a mile and a half, and within half an hour the sky, with no exaggeration, turned black with planes.

I read after the war that there were somewhere in the region of two and a half thousand heavy and medium bombers including British, Americans and Canadians.

They rained down a total of four thousand tonnes of explosives. We could feel the shock waves all the way back where we were, a good mile off; it was frightening. I had never seen anything like it in my life. Those aeroplanes just kept on a-coming and a-coming, by God, and they bombed for about an hour and a half without stopping. When it was all over the smoke rose around two thousand feet in the air.

Operation Cobra, as it was called, was the largest tactical ground support bombing in history at the time, starting at about 0940 and ending at 1100 on July 25, 1944.

The Yankee war correspondent Ernie Pyle, who, as you would expect, had a way with words, described it later, saying, 'The thundering motors in the sky, and the roar of the bombs, filled all the space for noise on earth and seemed to destroy all of the world up ahead of us.'

*

We were just young fellas, aged nineteen or twenty, and we were confronted with this carnage.

Hedgerows, buildings, cattle, horses and people, both civilians and soldiers, had been blown to hell but a lot of German tanks and a lot of German infantry had been blown up with them. Mercifully you didn't have a lot of time to look as there were still concentrations of German tanks and troops waiting for us and we sure didn't want to disappoint.

Chapter 7

Spearhead

The idea, after all that bombing, was that we moved forward as quickly as possible; if we stagnated then we were in trouble again. And move we did, with such pace and ferocity that the 3rd Armoured Division became known as the Spearhead Division.

It was fairly common practice to give a division a name over and above its official title, such as the 3rd Armored Division of the 1st Army, and Spearhead had a tremendous amount of meaning because we were always out front, in touch with the enemy at all times, leading the fight, day and night.

The moniker was the brainchild of our General, Maurice Rose. As far as I was led to believe, he was very proud of the fact that the Division was moving along following the breakthrough in and around Saint-Lô, and that we were at the point of so much of the combat that was going on. We, in turn, were proud of the name and proud of our General.

General Patton's armoured infantry was called Hell on Wheels and General Rose thought, seeing as we were leading so much of the activity deeper into France, that he would call the 3rd Armored Division, Spearhead.

There are other divisions with special names that were given to them by their commands such as the 101st Airborne Division, known as the Screaming Eagles, and the 1st Infantry Division were The Big Red One, from the division's official shoulder patch, which was a red number 1. The British boys also had names that were fitting to the intensity of their involvement with the Germans, such as the Desert Rats following their heroic campaign in the deserts of North Africa.

*

Operation Cobra proved to be a success and, temporarily at least, it threw the German 7th Army into disarray, allowing us to bust out of the hedgerows. The bomb corridor was just wide enough to allow us to break through but they had bombed so heavily there were all sorts of craters and obstructions in the way.

We had to find a way of getting the vehicles around or over them. As there was no time or opportunity to build roads, we just had to move with what we had. We had a fairly large truck that carried around six to eight pieces of steel treadway, each ten to twelve-foot long and wide enough for a tank's track to cross. We would put one either side of the obstacle, and we would join several up if whatever we were crossing was longer. Using this method, our tanks could cross almost anything.

When crossing rivers we had pontoons that we used to inflate. They were very big and powerful enough to hold up two pieces of treadway on either side. We would have ropes attached to the pontoons and guys further up the riverbank would hold them in position while we secured them.

Another bridge that was very useful was the Bailey bridge, which was a land-based pre-fabricated wood and steel truss bridge that was developed by the British. Again we could put them up fairly quickly, without a crane, and they could handle a tank and get things moving.

*

It didn't have to be a full-blown bridge; we also laid treadways for tanks to cross soft ground, a ditch, crater or a stream. Trix, The Greek and me helped put up many of them after the enemy had been pushed back. They were vital to keep the 3rd Armored Division moving forward. Most of the time we were putting up bridges you were exposed to mortar fire, small arms fire, the works, usually coming from the other side of the river. We were protected by our own infantry, which did a marvellous job amid the intense German firepower, yet it was still an extremely dangerous situation to be in.

Having busted out of those damned hedgerows we were moving like a well-oiled machine and there was a method to our movement that enabled us to keep that spearhead pushing forward.

Right out front were the reconnaissance guys in jeeps, and boy did they have some guts. They were small units and they were always looking for the enemy. They would inch forward, right up to the German line, and report back whatever was going on up there to the Division's Command Post. The lifespan of the recons, as you can imagine being right out in front, wasn't very long at all because they were literally in constant touch with the enemy, all the way through. When they stopped we came up behind them and took over and gave them a break. Then they would go off again and find where the Germans were once more.

Also, the recon guys would often quite literally run into the minefields. They would then get on the radio and say 'Minefield up ahead' and they would give the coordinates on the map. It cost some of their lives, but the information and intelligence they supplied saved many more.

*

Up above them were the fly-guys in their Piper Cub aircraft; they did a tremendous job.

Those small two-man aircraft kept in contact with the recon guys and constantly fed information back to us. The Piper Cubs were a constant target because the Germans knew what they were about. They used to come in low to take a look at what was happening and a lot of them were shot down by rifle and automatic rapid fire. But thank God for them because they could alert us, saying things like 'You have this on your left, this on your right, this is up ahead.' They gave us a big advantage and saved a lot of lives and equipment.

The tanks were next. After all these years I don't recall too much about the kind of tanks. There were a hell of a lot of Shermans—the official record shows that there were some two hundred and thirty medium tanks in Spearhead—and I do recall a newer version arriving on the scene after a few months. They were lower to the ground, the armament was bigger and stronger, but as to the specifics I was no expert; to me a tank was a tank.

In battle, many times when they were moving, we would climb aboard the back and get a ride forward. The commander inside would know we were there. It was always comforting to see our tanks when you were in combat but, to be honest, we didn't work with them directly very often. When we did the number would vary from six to eight to around thirty depending on the layout of the combat situation. I only saw one major tank battle. It was up in northern France. I had been working with the infantry and we stopped because to our right were a whole bunch, maybe twenty-five to thirty, of our tanks in combat, tank to tank with the Germans.

I didn't know any of the tankers personally but we were a band of brothers; they were part of us—it was the 3rd Armored Division, 23rd Armored Engineers, 36th Armored Infantry, we were all Armored. We worked with them when it was called for, whether that was riding with them or hollering information at them; when they had the flap down and the guy would have his head out, we would holler 'Heavy stuff down there,' and indicate the direction with our arms.

Personally, I never wanted to be a tanker. I was more at ease working with explosives, building bridges and acting as infantry. I didn't fancy tanks because you are too confined; to my way of thinking, if you got hit inside that tank your head was tinsel. But I had a lot of respect for the guys who did; they were one hundred per cent American and there to do a job as a tanker and as a soldier. My hat went off to them many, many times because they were brave soldiers.

We did everything we could to facilitate the movements of those tanks. If there was an obstruction, a crater or a bridge out, we would be there making sure they could keep moving. Part of the job of an engineer was to stand out in front of that tank and direct them in; most of the time it was done under a considerable amount of enemy fire. Yes, it was risky but it was all risky.

Then came the TDs (Tank Destroyers): they had a real heavy gun. The difference between it and a tank was that it was bigger, it had a much more powerful gun and the ammunition was specifically designed to take out tanks.

The tanks were smaller and more manoeuvrable, and while they were capable of tank-to-tank fighting, sometimes, if they came across a stubborn situation, they would call the TDs in. They were trained for what we called stationary aiming. If the word came from recon that there was a group of tanks up ahead then the TDs would move in with our regular tanks and when they saw the German tanks they could zero-in and they had the right kind of ammunition, the right velocity to do some real damage; they were specially trained for that kind of thing.

*

The 36th Armored Infantry Regiment were right up there alongside the tanks and often in combat, in the towns and villages, they would be leading the way. When not riding the tanks, or in amongst them fighting, they would travel in half-tracks. Their job was to help protect those tanks and also to move with them into combat; they were right on the front line of things. They took heavy casualties as you might expect and lost something like seven different commanding officers but they were brave and fearless—I had the privilege of fighting alongside them many times.

*

The Engineers were at the back of the tanks and the infantry but when we were called upon we would go up ahead of them both, near the recon, and do whatever we had to do in terms of the road condition, mines, explosives, that kind of thing.

We travelled in our open-top half-tracks. Inside would be enough room for a squad: twelve men, five sitting on each side, the guy on the .50 calibre in the turret and the driver. We had ammunition and explosives in there, whatever we needed to get the job done.

We would regularly have to leave the half-track and go off on foot, either into combat or on some mission with the infantry. With a squad of infantry there were usually two engineers. When we were out on patrol we travelled near the back but we would have to go up there and take a look and do whatever we had to do, if called upon. Anything to do with mines or explosives the sergeant would shout, 'Engineers', sending the word back down the line to us. We would run forward and take care of whatever they had found.

Then you had the Signal Corps who had to lay

telephone lines down to keep communications going forward so those up front could call back to the command post to explain what was happening.

It may sound like a harmless job but they lost a lot of guys climbing up those doggone poles laying a line. They were in sight of the frontline all the time and came under a lot of fire. Spearhead kept moving so the line had to keep moving so that communication was going back to the tankers and Division Command.

*

The medics were always on the line with us. Each platoon, around forty-eight men, had their own medic who stayed really close. They were very courageous; they would be right out there as the guys got shot or lost an arm or a leg or whatever was happening. They immediately took care of anyone who needed them, regardless of any risk to themselves.

If someone was hit, and we were close enough, we sometimes stopped and helped, but you usually had to leave it to the medic; that was his job. If everybody stopped to pay attention to what was going on with their buddies the line wouldn't move forward. We were taught that we had to go forward and that the medics would take care of any wounded; they knew what they were doing—we didn't. We got on with the job we were supposed to do and what we were there for.

We did carry some basic first aid stuff that we used if there was no one else around and we had the time. We were taught to immediately sprinkle a sulphur powder on any open wound to prevent infection. It was in a little package that we had in a pouch; it was a white powder and was fairly effective if you got hit. If the wound was pretty nasty we whipped out the sulphur, put it on and there was a bandage that we wrapped around it. The Greek used one when he got hit by a small piece of shrapnel in the side of his neck and so did some of my other buddies who had some pretty nasty wounds. I used it myself when I took some shrapnel to the knee—it was wonderful stuff.

Fortunately we didn't need to patch ourselves up too often, as our medics were outstandingly brave individuals. They didn't have any firearms to return fire but if a man was wounded he got attention right there and then. They saved countless lives due to their quick action in battle.

Sometimes a guy would be out there in a field, just hollering because he had been hit. I can remember our medic, he was from Wisconsin, hearing this guy screaming for help and he went out there. We gave him protection because the Germans would shoot them even though they had a Red Cross sign on their arms; whether that was by design or just because it was in a combat situation, we don't know.

I saw a couple of medics wounded. Keep in mind that it wasn't all small-arms fire; shrapnel was everywhere and it sure didn't discriminate. When an artillery piece was fired, the explosives were set to go off in mid-air. That was bloody terrible because you would get a bursting in the air—not high but low—and it would take out a whole bunch of guys. I have seen chunks of shrapnel as big as your fist going straight through a guy. Once I took a guy down to the aid station, he had lost a chunk of his foot. There were a lot of guys laying down there all butchered up, wounded and dying.

*

Then came the artillery and, behind them, the anti-aircraft guns. The artillery had a range of two or three miles. Recon would talk to the guys in the Piper Cub and they would talk to the artillery and give them positions. Also, if we met with stubborn resistance we would call in the artillery. We did this a lot. Sometimes it was marginally effective but most times it was very effective. The sergeant would say, 'They are calling in the artillery, lay down.'

You could hear those shells going over your head. It was a relief to know that you had artillery there as backup. On the other hand, when the Germans sent incoming mail, as we called it, the noise was very frightening indeed, depending upon where you were when those shells came in. I have heard that sound so many times, and you know when it's about to land because it changes sound and kind of fizzles out.

Working closely with the artillery were the spotters and they too had a risky job keeping fairly close to the action. They had walkie-talkies, which were huge, but they also had radiotelephones. The first time I saw them I wondered who the hell they were but our sergeant said that they were spotters for the artillery. Keep in mind, when we were moving into a village the Germans had their own spotters up in the church towers who had to be taken out.

*

The anti-aircraft guns were another comfort even though there was very little Luftwaffe activity during the day as the Allies ruled the skies, but sometimes at night they would put in an appearance, announcing themselves with parachute flares followed by anti-personnel mines that were designed to explode in the air, which was very bloody nasty.

*

Then you had Division CP (Command Post) and maintenance, which was extremely important. You may think the maintenance and repair guys had it fairly easy, way back in the rear, but sometimes they had to go up to the front to get a tank or half-track moving. Much of the time, these guys were working under direct enemy fire.

Right at the rear were supplies that were essential, especially the food. The American Army sure liked to eat. We lived on K rations, which came in a package about the size of one of those cartons of two hundred cigarettes but a little wider and thicker. They were covered in a certain kind of grease, making them waterproof. We carried a load of them in the half-track. When you opened it up you had a can of cheese, a small can of spam, some crackers, four cigarettes, some matches and a few pieces of toilet paper.

In addition you had a ten-in-one, a box of all kinds of chow, done in a certain way so moisture couldn't get into it. Inside was soup and lots of stuff so the whole squad could sit around and have a bit of meal, which didn't happen very often.

The name for the average American soldier was explained to me like this—your army boots were general issue, your shirts were general issue, your whole self was general issue, so you became a GI; that's my understanding of the term.

*

I was in C Squad of C Platoon in E Company. You go from a squad to a platoon, with four squads in a platoon. In charge of each squad is a sergeant and a corporal, with a lieutenant and staff sergeant taking control over the whole platoon.

There would be four or five platoons, with one being what we called headquarters—they did all the paperwork and things like that—in a company. The lieutenants reported to a captain, which is the next level, and/or a major. That's the way it ran as far as I can remember.

Then four or five companies made up a battalion and, in turn, three or four battalions made a regiment and another three or four regiments made up a division.

We were organised operationally into task forces known as Combat Command A, led by General Doyle Hickey, and Combat Command B under General Truman Boudinot. I was in Command A.

They each had their own combat force of tanks, infantry, engineers, artillery—two separate Spearheads that worked in tandem with each other. They were ready to move in whatever direction General Rose wanted. Each command was given separate orders to take this village or this bridge.

They carried out different tasks but were always coordinating. They were two different teams with the same objective—to take out the enemy.

Sometimes we would be in the thick of it leading the charge while Command B would be in reserve, and vice versa.

*

As a GI, I pretty much spent the majority of my time attached to that half-track surrounded by the same bunch of guys, a squad of twelve men. Although I was in this squad for months and months I sometimes went off on assignments with other infantry units. Sometimes in the heat of battle you would end up being with another unit for one reason or other and you kind of stayed with them until you could move back up to your own outfit.

Our sergeant was called Robert Foster and he was from Memphis, Tennessee. At twenty-three or twenty-four he was a few years older than most of the guys. He was a leader but also a guy you could talk to and reason with; that was one of his biggest assets.

Our corporal was Harold Graves but we all called him Zeek. He was a farm boy from Pontiac, Illinois.

Zeek was fair and very aware of battle situations and would throw his whole self into combat. He was one hell of a good soldier in my estimation. Zeek was a big fella but bear in mind I was probably the smallest guy in the outfit; I was just a tiny Welshman, built close to the ground. Trix was just a little bit bigger than me and The Greek was a little bit bigger again. They always bragged about that and I used to tell them to bugger off. When it came down to it, it was not how big you were but the guts that you had to get up and have a go at those sonsofbitches that were shooting at you. It was constant. The environment was always dangerous. Whether you were engaged in fighting or disengaged, you still had the mines to deal with and booby-traps they'd set for you, so there was always danger.

Much of what went on in these combat situations was down to the non-commissioned officers—the corporals and sergeants. I'm not saying that our officers weren't in it. They certainly weren't sitting back directing this and that, they were in it up to their necks, but as GIs we mostly got ordered about by Sergeant Foster and Zeek.

Sometimes you had to play it by ear. When you were on the move you saw situations, and as a soldier, you had to take care of it. You would whistle or you would signal with your hand by pointing your finger and the rest of the guys would pick it up: 'There's action there, be careful.'

Our lieutenant was a guy called Russell Norwood Junior. He was a leader in every sense of the word. He was not precious about his rank as an officer; he was in my opinion a soldier's officer. He was from down south, Louisiana, and he used to call me Limey. We would call him Sir or Lieutenant or use his name, depending upon where we were and what we were doing.

Lieutenant Norwood was also a little older than the rest of us guys, probably around twenty-six to twenty-eight, and he was the kind of man who would be right there in the line of fire. We lost too many officers in combat because they were Americans to the core. It was the country they were fighting for, their involvement, their commitment, the job of soldiering rested upon their shoulders and they knew it and they stepped up to the plate time and time again, by God.

They would be a natural target as they were standing up there directing operations at the edge of it. On the back of a second lieutenant's helmet was a white stripe. The reason for it was so we could recognise who the officers were by looking at their backs but the Germans wouldn't know that they were officers because they were looking at them from the front. Most of our officers had university training and us buck privates looked up to them as knowing everything. We had respect for our officers but we wouldn't take any crap from them.

Most of the guys could have gone to officer training school if they had wanted; I couldn't have, I was too stupid. That suited me fine, as I never wanted to be an officer. I just wanted to be one of the guys; too many of the officers were getting killed. I said to myself, 'Limey, you don't want this, there's already too much going on around you without poking your head in as an officer.'

*

Our driver was Melville Sharp from La Salle, Illinois. He was a good mechanic and he knew about engines, their capacity and what they could and could not do. When I stood in the half-track's turret, on that .50 calibre machinegun, he sat to the left of where my feet were. If

I wanted him to turn right or left, so I could get into a better position to do what I had to do, I would just reach over and kick him on the shoulder and shout 'Right. Right. Right.' Also if I saw German aeroplanes coming in to attack us I would holler down, 'Take cover, aeroplanes.'

He could see out of slits in the armoured shutters. He didn't have the entire thing open in combat, and he could see things that I couldn't see if I was facing an opposite direction. He had my back, as it were.

He would shout, 'Limey, to your right.'

And I would swing around. If I hadn't have swung around I wouldn't be here now. There were a number of times when his sharp sight and ability to size up a situation saved my life.

*

A soldier's day on the line is split into two: before combat and during combat. You had to be extremely aware of what was happening around you all the time. The reader needs to keep in mind the fluid situation that we were in. Like other combat troops, and there were hundreds of thousands of them, we were dependent upon other human beings around us in trying to move forward.

Our main objective was to move ahead and take whatever position the Germans were holding at that time, whether a farmhouse, a village or part of a city.

140

Then we would stop and hold the line, replacements would come up for the men who had got killed, the wounded were taken to hospital, we stocked up on gas and food and then we would move forward again.

We normally tried to move in the daylight hours but at times it was at night. We would reach a point where we couldn't go too much further because of the logistics involved and what was in front of us.

As with the hedgerows, you got your sleep wherever and whenever you could get it; but unlike those damned hedgerows the terrain was slightly different. Although still rural, there were more villages and small towns. If you took that village or farmhouse there would be an opportunity for you to sleep undercover. There were times when you would fight like hell to take a village so you would have somewhere to sleep that night. We would also sleep in barns with the animals if the option were available to us; failing that you would either put your head down in the half-track, if it was close by, or in a foxhole.

When we came to a standstill and Sergeant Foster told us that we would be there for a while you would immediately get out your small foldaway shovel and start digging. I had wisely teamed up with Trix because being a coalminer he was like a machine; he could dig a foxhole faster than I could breathe. He would dig it and we would share it. You would get used to doing it the right way. You would use the soil dug out to build up a mound around the hole and look around for pieces of tin or wood to throw over the top to make a roof. The central idea was the artillery at times would explode in mid-air and all that shrapnel would come down hot and heavy and at speed on top of you. Also, you didn't want the foxhole very wide for that reason.

Sergeant Foster would draw up a roster for guard duty. You would sleep head to foot and, of course, you had no problem getting to sleep—as soon as your head hit the ground you would be asleep, you were so tired.

Me, Trix and The Greek had a secret weapon when it came to sleeping under the stars— sleeping bags. I'm not talking the down-filled deal you see today but the homemade canvas variety.

I'm not proud of how we came by them but they made a real difference to sleeping rough. We 'acquired' them back in England following a night out on the town in Tisbury. We were on our way back to the base in Fonthill Bishop when we passed the backyard of a pub. Trix stopped and pointed out a large tarpaulin covering up some barrels.

He said, 'Guys, if we could have that we could make ourselves sleeping bags that we could fold up and carry in our backpacks. It could come in real handy in the weeks ahead.'

'You've got a good idea there,' I said.

It was the one and only time that we were really out of line, but we stole it, or commandeered it as Trix said.

Back on the base we cut it up into a handful of strips. One of the guys had a sail maker's needle and we said, 'If you do the sewing we will give you a sleeping bag.'

Of course we felt real guilty about pinching it, but we needed it more than those barrels. Those tarp pieces turned out to be a real lifesaver when we were hunkered down in the trenches in the pouring rain for days on end. In our prayers, we often thanked the landlord for his unknown generosity.

*

When you move into a combat situation you realise that the life of a soldier changes with the understanding that at any moment you could be hurt, perhaps killed, and you take onto yourself the responsibility of looking after yourself and your buddies.

Also, when you are in barracks you have all the amenities such as toilets and showers but then comes the day when you move out into the field. Back in England, when we were stationed in Fonthill Bishop, we moved out into the woods and our pup tents for three or four days to prepare us for living out of that environment.

The everyday inspections you used to get back in the barracks about cleanliness go out of the window because you are on the move and there is no consideration for toilets, eating or anything like that because the most important thing is staying alive and completing the objective. You eat your K rations, or a ten-in-one with your buddies if you are holding the line, and take a nap whenever you can. If you want to go to the toilet you go off into the woods; sometimes you would dig a hole but most of the time you just didn't have the time, or if you've taken a village you use the toilet there. There was no embarrassment in going off into the woods and doing what you had to do. Not like when I was back in the various camps where there were usually around thirty toilets in a large room in the toilet block and no partitions. You are sitting there doing what comes naturally and there are around twenty-nine other guys doing the same. Now that is kind of embarrassing, but you get used to it.

Between the dust in summer and the mud that was everywhere in winter we were caked in dirt and grime pretty much all the time. I have a photograph in my possession of the guys posing for the camera somewhere in northern France and we look like we had never seen a bar of soap in our lives. You didn't pay much attention to the way you looked or the way you felt in terms of personal hygiene; we would go for maybe ten days without shaving, it wasn't important, you never combed your hair, you would be too busy. Most of the time it was strong opposition from the Germans in terms of firepower. This is what you had to contend with on a day-to-day basis, and we really didn't have time to worry about the niceties of shaving and washing.

There was one neat trick that we did manage to pull off once in a while where we would run a jeep around a bit to get hot water from its radiator so you could have a shave; but not in winter because there would be antifreeze in there.

*

Combat was exhausting physically and certainly mentally. Even being in so-called reserve is taxing; you are fully combat-ready and on the heels of whatever is going on up there. If they need you, you go in, you are ready. When we were in some heavy stuff and needed help, the reserve unit was always there. On a handful of occasions—in all honesty I can only recall two or three during our time in France and Belgium—we were sent back down the column for rest and recuperation. We went back off the line and were replaced by infantry for two days.

*

The time spent in that rest camp, which had large showers and toilet facilities, as well as halfway decent bunks, was heaven on earth.

We could have a shower, good chow, candy, ice cream, doughnuts, you name it. You didn't know it was going to happen, you would just hear, 'Okay guys, we are going back for R&R. Move. Get out. Get on the truck.'

It also afforded us the opportunity to sit around and relax and write letters home, something that never happened on the line. When you were in the army you were allowed to write but then it would go to the lieutenant and he would send it off for censorship. I wrote to Dr Race and his family back in New York and my family back in Swansea, explaining that I was okay, but I was never a big letter writer, because most of my time in St David's School had been spent sitting in the corner with the dunce cap on—I was no good at writing.

Trix had a girlfriend back in Pennsylvania who he would drop a line to once in a while but he wasn't much good at writing and spelling either. The Greek was the same, saying that if he was to write to every girl he knew he would have spent all day writing. He was like a sailor with a girl in every port.

Such rest times were more than welcome because combat is a terrible thing; your life is on the line constantly and there are things that you see that no man should be expected to witness. We were after all still very young, almost children, but in war you have to grow up fast.

The stench of death was never far away; animals were lying around dead and stinking. Normally you would find civilians alongside because they would have been trying to protect their animals so they died as well. Bodies were lying around that couldn't be attended to. Some of our own boys were mixed in there amongst the Germans;

that was very difficult for a lot of us guys to get used to. The smell of death was a terrible thing, there's no doubt about that, and I have never forgotten it.

*

Such was the mobile nature of Spearhead we would often bypass villages and towns, and it led us to being surrounded on many occasions and at times we hit considerable German resistance. This is when the 36th Armored Infantry would go into action with the support of the tanks to annihilate those pockets of resistance. Even the supplies and the administration people would be engaged in the fighting at times: whether you were a cook or an infantryman, it didn't make any difference, you still picked up that rifle and engaged the enemy.

We were always mindful of the fact that we were in combat and could have been hit at any time, with bullets, shrapnel, artillery, you name it, because that was the nature of combat. Fortunately for me the men that I talked to, that I fought alongside, that got wounded or died, were good people and true heroes and I will never forget them.

When you are talking about American soldiers, the whole band of us, whether you are infantry, engineers, cooks or bottle washers, we were all buddies. If you were in uniform then you were not a stranger. The best way to describe the feeling was a kind of esprit de corps—a common spirit of comradeship, enthusiasm and devotion to a cause.

That comradeship played a vital part in us moving forward as an armoured division deep into enemy territory all the time.

Family

From left to right: my sister Edwina, my mother, me aged 5, my grandfather and my baby sister Eunice who died of diphtheria before her first birthday.

New Recruit

Fresh from my basic training at Fort Leonard Wood Missouri.

The Three Musketeers

Limey, Trix and the Greek!

Graduation

That's me (front row second from right) with the guys after basic training in Fort Leonard Wood Missouri.

Take Off

Me test piloting a German fighter plane in Paderborn.

Platoon Buddies

Our driver Sharp is sat on the hood, Trix is leaning next to the front wheel while the Greek is second from the right.

Tom Cruise

Standing on the hood of our half-track somewhere in Belgium.

Spearhead Selfie

Me and my buddies, Trix is behind me, on the half-track as part of the column pushing through what looks like Belgium.

Unrecognisable

Me (second right) and my buddies greeted by locals after liberating Namur despite being caked in mud and dust.

Sweethearts and Partners

Me and Maggie, the love of my life in Swansea before the new millennia.

Return Journey

I made an emotional return to Omaha Beach in 2009.

Pals

Me and my biographer Geraint Thomas.

Finally We Meet

Meeting The Greek's wife, Shirley Kallas, in 2011.

Patriot

I may be Welsh but I am also a proud American citizen.

Buckingham Palace

Me and Maggie meeting the Queen in June 2013.

Top Brass

Meeting the British Prime Minister David Cameron as part of the VE Day celebrations in London.

Legion

I am proud to be a member of both the American and British legions.

Merci Beaucoup

Receiving the Ordre national de la Légion d'honneur from the French in the US Embassy in London in the summer of 2018.

Chapter 8

The Falaise Gap

Spearhead kept on moving forward into August with very little let-up in the action. The breakout had allowed us to get into some really serious combat with the Germans and that led to the Falaise Gap.

Now Trix, The Greek and me, along with the rest of the guys in the 3rd Armored Division, were involved in all five major campaigns in the European theatre of war, beginning with the D-Day landings and the Battle of Normandy, carrying on with the conquest for northern France, through to the Rhineland, the Ardennes, which included the brutal Battle of the Bulge, and the fight for central Germany. We were right there on the front line in the thick of it as history was unfolding before our eyes but, at the time, we didn't have a clue as to the significance of it all.

Today you will find whole books written on individual battles such as the Falaise Gap or the Battle of the Bulge, but while it was happening we knew nothing other than the fact that we had a job to do, which was to take out the Germans and move forward and to keep doing that until the end of the war. We were in places that we didn't even know were places because we were moving so fast and switching direction from day to day; none of us could tell you whether we were in France or Belgium; the language sounded the same, and most of the road signs had been removed.

The bigger picture was just not available to us and there wasn't time to study where we were or what we were doing. I didn't have a map. Not that we cared much: Spearhead was part of a front that was maybe thirty miles wide but as an individual you are only aware of, and concerned with, what is going on around you; all that matters is keeping yourself and your buddies alive... and inflicting as much damage as you can on the Germans.

I now know that the battle of the Falaise Gap was fought for almost two weeks in the middle of August 1944. Back then its significance was lost on us but the violence, devastation and bloodshed was plain for all to see; those of us who were unlucky enough to be there would revisit the carnage in our nightmares for years to come.

*

Following the D-Day landings the Allied campaign was split in two. The British, Polish, Canadian and the Free French units were to push south via Caen to Falaise while the Americans would push west along the Normandy coast to Brittany and liberate the major cities and towns there before moving south towards Brest. However, US General Omar Bradley, who had command of our ground forces in western Europe, believed he could spare some of his men to push inland towards Falaise. He believed it was possible to trap the Germans if his men pushed from the south and the other Allies, under Field Marshal Bernard Montgomery, pushed from the north. There was a lot of respect for Montgomery amongst the US troops because he would get on his feet and say what he thought; he was an outstanding general.

All this led to tens of thousands of soldiers along with tanks, half-tracks and field guns flooding into that small part of France around Falaise. Strategically, if the Germans lost that battle we would take control of Normandy and the route to crossing the River Seine and the prospect of liberating Paris was truly on. Any delays, on the other hand, would allow the Germans to bring reinforcements up from southern France, so, as always, we had to move and move fast.

For days the Germans kept us from linking up and blocking their escape. Hitler had refused to allow his army to turn tail and run and demanded a counter attack. That in turn created an opportunity for us to trap the entire German presence in that part of France.

Eventually, after days of some of the bloodiest fighting of the war, the German commander in Normandy, Gunther von Kluge, ignored Hitler and told his troops to get the hell out of there.

At first they started to get away because, despite our best efforts to close in on both sides of them, there was still a small avenue between Falaise and Argentan; it was about thirty miles wide but it was getting smaller and smaller as time went by, although it never fully closed. The truth was that Allied Commanders were worried that Allied soldiers could get killed by friendly fire if we got too close to the British and Canadians. Historians claim that the top brass just weren't prepared to risk an embarrassing situation and that led to a small part of the gap remaining open and thousands of Germans getting through.

After all these years, one of the things I do remember is that the closer we got to the British, the heavier the fighting with the enemy became. The Germans weren't stupid, they realised that they were being pocketed and they fought like hell to avoid it. It was intense and fierce because they knew that they had had it if they didn't get through. Rather than face the shame of surrender they were prepared to fight to the death.

And amongst them were the fearsome and fanatical SS Panzer divisions and crack paratrooper regiments. Whenever you ran into the SS you were running into a brick wall. You could always tell the difference because they were much more determined; they just didn't give up. They were committed as special troops to Hitler, they were committed to the oath they had taken to their Führer and they died taking care of what they had to take care of. They were very stubborn and very aggressive; in a sense they were outstanding soldiers, they knew their business, they knew soldiering, they had been at war for years.

We did take some SS prisoners. They didn't want to be taken prisoner but we took them and we kept guard of them. Back in the rear we had our intelligence officers who would want to talk to them. Sometimes the infantry were given special assignments to bring back prisoners for interrogation. Usually, two combat engineers were assigned to these squads in case they ran into mines, booby traps or other explosives. Trix, The Greek and I were on some of those missions. They were some of the most dangerous times we faced in combat and I can't begin to tell you how frightening they were. Getting back to our lines didn't mean safety by any means, but it was still a huge relief.

All that said, the British and American boys knew that we had a job to do, which was to take them out so that they couldn't get at us later in Germany. We worked very well with the British; they were fearless, very committed and damned good at what they did. The Americans had a lot of respect for them because at times all of us, forgive the vernacular, were in deep shit; we depended upon each other for certain things and we worked together.

The battlefield was mostly open countryside with a few rural towns and villages. We were moving through

153

farmland, we were moving through villages and small towns, whatever obstacles were in the way. Although the smaller country lanes still had hedgerows it wasn't the same kind of jungle as the Bocage country, thank God, but that's not to say it wasn't equally as bad.

Once again, the Allied planes bombed the crap out of the Germans to soften them up and when we moved in we made our numbers count. Once the Germans had decided to make a run for it—on heavily congested roads—the situation became a bit like shooting fish in a barrel. Our artillery occupied the high ground; hundreds of those guns blasted the lines of retreating Germans all to hell on the open ground below; it was sheer carnage.

As it unfolded we had no idea of the vast number of German troops in that pocket. All we knew was that the resistance was getting tougher and tougher. If our lieutenant said we had to take that hill or village we would do it, but if we thought that it was a strategic point, then you can be damn sure the Germans also knew it and they wouldn't let it go without a fight. Then once you took it you had to secure it—just taking it wasn't enough.

All the time the Piper Cubs were up above directing our artillery over our heads into the middle of what the hell was going on. The action from the Germans trying to get out of there was fierce, there's no doubt about it, and I saw a lot of our boys getting wounded or killed, but each time we took a loss of life, we made damn sure the Germans took a loss of life in return.

Not only was the engagement very heavy, with a lot of lives lost on both sides, the Germans lost a lot of their transportation; either destroyed by us or sabotaged by themselves. The Germans were very short of fuel and we saw large numbers of burnt-out tanks, personnel carriers and other vehicles, which they had destroyed during their withdrawal rather than leave them for the Allies. The whole area was littered with the remnants of an army in retreat.

The Germans at times were using horses to pull their guns, still trying to escape. We did think it kind of strange but realised that they were trying to get their cannons and other equipment into a position where they could use them against us again, so we trained our .50 calibre guns on them then and opened fire.

Their vehicles got trapped, one behind the other, in those roads and country lanes, and while they were easy targets for our tanks, it caused another heap of trouble. The lanes would be chock-a-block with overturned and burnt-out German trucks, jeeps and even horses that had got killed, so we couldn't get through.

As engineers we would have to direct our tanks. If it was a car or something they could go straight over the top, but they could get hung up on the bigger stuff. You also had to bear in mind that American GIs, either wounded or dead, may be laying amongst the wreckage, so we had to be pretty careful. We would look for a better way that we could get our vehicles around but we also had to be mindful that the enemy might be behind a truck or someplace waiting to fire at us. We would move rather slowly, cautiously, but we would move all the same and not sit still.

Although I had tasted combat up in Isigny and Saint-Lô, it was nothing compared to the ferocity of the German Army trying to get out through the Falaise Gap; it was intense and it went on for days. The Germans were ruthless with the civilians coming through there because they wanted to get out and we made sure that we kept closing this gap; they were like a cornered tiger, unpredictable and fierce.

They staged a rear-guard action with the main idea being, in my opinion, to get as many troops as possible out of Normandy and to try and get to Paris and regroup their forces.

*

A lot of the time I was riding in the half-track. We were moving forward with our tanks and there was a hell of a lot of our artillery going over our heads. I was up in that turret with my .50 calibre machine gun, the rest of the guys were down below. My job was to make sure that I took out as many of the enemy as I could. I was able to see what was going on and directed my fire. Keep in mind that ours was just one half-track, we had about fifteen of them with these guns doing the same thing.

156

I came very close to getting hit on a number of occasions and I saw other guys operating .50 calibres getting killed. I had the opportunity to duck down, which I did sometimes, but then you would pop up again, slowly, to see what was going on, and you would start firing again. You sure did use a lot of ammunition rather quickly. The ammunition belt is hanging down on the right hand side and Sharp, the driver, had these .50 calibre cases next to him. I would shout, 'Ammo,' and I would rip out the used belt and he would pass me the new ammo without even slowing down.

*

At times a tracer bullet would come out, usually every fifteen bullets or so; it would light up red for it had a special substance on it that would show the bullet moving. You would see the tracers from the other guys and you would know what was going on.

You weren't firing all the time but all the time you were looking and reporting down to the driver below, telling him things like right or left. At times that gun would get so damn hot it would jam on me; it was very scary because I had lost my main firepower and protection. All I could do was let it cool off while I carried on with my rifles or the Colt .45 which I carried strapped to my leg.

While you could say being on that .50 calibre was

one of the riskier jobs in the platoon there were no heroics; it was just a job to do, and, as they say, somebody's got to do it. I had my buddies down there in the half-track and I was always aware of them; their lives depended on little Limey and that gun because I was the one who could see what was going on.

*

The half-track wasn't really suited to close combat in a village, town or city. It would be too easily tied down or zeroed in on by a well-placed German gun, so often a point would come where we would stop and get out and fight alongside the infantry. You made sure you had plenty of ammo, some hand grenades, or whatever the hell you needed, and you always carried plenty of water.

When the half-track stopped, we would get out the back and immediately fall to the ground until we found out what was going on. Sometimes we would have to crawl underneath. There was a door at the back and one on the driver's side. My turret and me were on the passenger side. I would be the last one out as I was dedicated to the .50 calibre covering the other guys. Sometimes I would just stay there and use the .50; it was an individual decision taken at the time. I did not have time to think properly, I just reacted to what was going on and trusted in the Almighty that I reacted in a positive way and could handle it.

Away from the villages and towns, the battlefields of the Gap, with their open areas of land, made for perfect tank country and we faced a hell of a lot of those Panzers coming at us. When you are looking at a tank firing, it's not firing at you per se, it's firing at something bigger than you, but those tanks also had machine guns on them and they were looking at Limey and his buddies and trying to take us out.

It usually took a tank destroyer or another tank to take a tank out, but there were times when the German tanks were so close we could throw in grenades at their treads. Many times the situation called for taking the M1, putting a rocket grenade on the end of it, and firing at the treads of the tanks. I didn't take out many tanks but the ones I did take out were with my bazooka or my M1 rifle grenade.

A bazooka was like a tube, about five-foot long, which I would rest on my shoulder and slap my cheek up against the side to sight it. Trix would be behind me to jam in the explosive and he would shout, 'Okay?'

I would say, 'Yeah,' and he would get out of the way from behind and slap me on my back to let me know that it was safe to fire.

You didn't have time to think, you just fired. If you scored a hit you damaged it pretty darn good so it couldn't move. As the Germans tried to climb out you would shoot them. If it did move, you tried to get off another shot at it. With the M1 it would either bounce off or it would be effective. If it didn't work you got the hell out of the way or found a hole to jump into.

*

A lot of Germans surrendered during the heat of combat when they realised that they were being overwhelmed— this had been encouraged. I have in my possession a piece of paper which I saved that was dropped by British and American aeroplanes which basically said, in German and English, 'Hand this in and you won't be killed.' These guys had them in their hands.

I think hundreds of thousands of them were dropped but the first time I saw them was in the Gap. Even after the Gap there were still guys with them – I don't know if they were penalised for being caught in possession of them by their own officers but, knowing the German Army, you would be in some serious trouble.

Once they started waving those fliers around we would look to see if they had any guns and if they did you would point to it and say, 'Down.' They knew what we were talking about and they would throw it down. Then we would shout, 'Hände hoch.' (Hands up).

We were real careful because we hadn't forgotten the dirty tricks they played on us back in the hedgerows, where they would fall to the ground and reveal a machine gun. After making sure they were kosher you would point them through the line and the boys behind would take care of them. We didn't have the time to handle prisoners—there was more fighting up ahead. We gave them free passes through our lines and shouted 'Raus.' '(Out).'

At times the number of prisoners captured was quite considerable. They would form a line, two abreast. They had all been searched, every one of them, and they would be sent back under the guard of a handful of American soldiers, armed with automatic rifles, to the area designated for prisoners.

*

After a week or so of fierce fighting you noticed the heat of the battle getting cooler, the activity of the Germans slowed down and we felt as though it was coming to a close. We felt relieved but we were never ever off our guard.

The aftermath of the battle and its carnage was sickening to witness—even for the most battle-hardened of us. Martin Blumenson, the official US Army historical officer, once again, best described the sight.

He wrote, 'The carnage wrought in the final days was perhaps the greatest of the war. The roads and fields were littered with thousands of enemy dead and wounded, wrecked and burning vehicles, smashed artillery pieces, carts laden with the loot of France overturned and smouldering, dead horses and cattle swelling in the summer's heat.'

161

Other observers have since said that that battle was more brutal and costly, in terms of numbers and position for the Germans, than the infamous Battle of Stalingrad, while years later, President Dwight D Eisenhower went on record as saying, 'No other battlefield presented such a horrible sight of death, hell and total destruction.'

*

If I close my eyes, I can still see the wasteland that was left behind. The debris was still burning. Trucks, tanks and half-tracks with German bodies hanging out of them. Even horses were on fire. A considerable number of Germans were killed. I saw men in tanks with their heads blown off; a lot of dead Germans lying around killed in different ways, lots had lost limbs and suffered horrific burns.

I can remember villages where many civilians had been killed. Women and children had been caught up in the intensity of the battle and been killed because they happened to be in the way. Many were killed or wounded by shrapnel. The stench and the way people died were terrible. I remember I was in one place where a cat was sat on top of this dead person's chest eating away at the face. Exposure to this sort of thing took a huge emotional toll. I saw at least one situation where an infantry guy broke up completely; just couldn't take it anymore. The medics took him back down the column and I didn't see him again.

There was also the smell of cordite and diesel because of the tanks, and the natural smells of the countryside and its foliage, little trees and bushes. The stench of war overloads all of the senses.

When it became clear that the Germans had lost the major battle of the Falaise Gap, not surprisingly, Hitler relieved Kluge of his command and replaced him with General Walter Model. On his journey back to Germany, Kluge committed suicide; he knew that he would be blamed for the defeat in Normandy. If the Americans thought that a general wasn't doing his job they would replace him and explain the reason why; Hitler, on the other hand, had them killed.

Again, after consulting the history books, I can tell you that although nearly a hundred thousand Germans escaped the pocket before it was all but closed towards the end of August, around fifty thousand were captured and ten thousand killed. In addition, three hundred and forty-four tanks and armoured vehicles, nearly two and a half thousand trucks and other vehicles, along with two hundred and fifty-two artillery pieces, were captured or destroyed. I read recently that local scrap dealers were still earning a living clearing the scrap metal from wrecked German armour over thirty years after the battle had ended.

Chapter 9

Northern France

Victory in the Falaise Gap had pretty much ended the Battle of Normandy but there was no time for celebrating; we had the Germans on the run and we carried straight on after those sonsofbitches.

Usually you would expect a bit of rest and recuperation after such a major battle but I don't remember much, just the continuation of combat. We were in full battle on their heels. Fellow engineers had constructed a bridge across the River Seine and the route to Paris was wide open.

Paris fell on August 25, 1944, fairly easily in comparison to the previous hundred miles or so, which felt as though each mile had been bought with blood.

Now such a big prize as liberating Paris was a real political hot potato and in the end General Eisenhower decided to leave it to the French, led by Charles de Gaulle, which was probably the right decision. It was a golden opportunity for the French people to see their leader coming back and to lift their spirits in the knowledge that the war was nearly over for them. De

Gaulle took the opportunity to declare himself the President of France once more; he had fled to Great Britain when the Germans invaded, although I don't think that Churchill was too fond of him. Anyway, once Paris had been liberated, he was presenting himself as the saviour of France.

I was initially disappointed because we were so close, but then I thought to myself, this is really a French matter, it was an opportunity for de Gaulle to speak to his people and thank the Free French for what they had done; so many of them had been killed. They had rifles and ammunition that, apparently, the British had dropped to them. I saw them in combat taking care of a lot of Germans who were offering pockets of resistance; they were certainly committed to rescuing their country.

There were some US troops that got to march down the Champs-Elysees of course but little Limey, Trix and The Greek just carried on doing what we did best and chased the Germans—just because Paris had been liberated that didn't mean that the German army had gotten the hell out of France.

All I can remember is being told that Paris was over yonder on our left as we were moving through. The British boys were on the other side of Paris so you had a combination of the Americans, British and Free French trying to clean up on the outskirts, which was where the main action was anyway. The destruction was quite intense and we were certainly engaged with the Germans all the way along that corridor outside of Paris; the intensity did not let up.

One of the things that come to mind quite definitely is that the Free French were out in their droves. They were quite demonstrative with their feelings on seeing the Americans come past their capital city. They showed their gratitude.

In turn we were grateful to them as the Free French intelligence was effective in identifying pockets of remaining German soldiers waiting to ambush our troops as we passed by. Keep in mind an armoured division just keeps moving and widening the gap for others to follow. The rear would spread out and take care of the mopping up, which at times was quite fierce. You can't make light of the mopping-up operations because that was a tremendous job. I talked to guys who were involved with the process in a number of the places that we had been through. It was nasty and the term mopping up doesn't really do justice to the serious nature and importance of the job.

After losing Paris I figured the Germans weren't too concerned with northern France; all they wanted was to get back to their homeland and make a last stand. As they were retreating they would set up a post to cover their soldiers going through. It was what you call rear-guard action, and then guys further along would set up another post to allow those first guys to get through; if they were still alive, that is.

It was often a suicide post; rear-guard action quite literally saw them giving their lives away to save their comrades. It gave the main body of their army the chance to move back into Germany while they stood there and took the brunt of the Allied forces that were moving into their territory.

When I say the Germans were on the run you may imagine a couple of dozen soldiers running away; it was not like that at all. It's a matter of tanks, trucks, half-tracks, guns being towed both by horses and mechanised stuff, and thousands of soldiers with their equipment, supplies and ammunition. It's usually a well-organised system of retreating. I saw it time and time again, as we would be right after them. And once again you saw a lot of vehicles that had been burnt because the Germans didn't have gasoline.

Our job as engineers was to make sure that the path for our advancing army was relatively mine-free; in essence our job was to make sure that things kept moving. We made sure that the pressure was constant on those bastards.

We would try to stay on the road the best we could because it was the fastest way, but then again the Germans knew this. They weren't stupid, so they would mine certain parts of the road. When one went off it would wound, hurt or kill our boys, or damage the two-and-a-half-tonne truck, half-track, jeep or tank.

When a mine went off the column would stop and

the word 'Engineers' would be passed back along the column. When it reached us we went forward to clear that stretch of road. We would take our bayonets or combat knives and push them gently into the soil and if we met resistance, we knew that something was there.

Then we would pull the bayonet out and come in on the other side to make sure that it wasn't just a stone. You could gauge the size of the object. Those teller mines were the size of a dinner plate about three inches thick; it was a very crude method but very effective. Nine times out of ten we knew whether it was a mine or not. Then we would scoop the dirt out around that mine and make it inoperable. It was a job we had to do with extreme care, and a lot of lives were depending on us. Personally, and I think my buddies felt the same, we didn't think of the danger that was involved in taking a mine out of the ground. We knew how to neutralise it, we knew that we had to be careful. It took extreme concentration; we could not afford the luxury of worrying or allowing our thoughts to wander from the job at hand.

The Germans were very clever at laying and camouflaging their mines, and often booby-trapped them. Clearing a minefield was always difficult and dangerous. When we had to do this at night, it was especially risky; and when the weather turned bad and we had rain, snow and cold it was even worse. We couldn't use gloves so our hands were freezing and clumsy, which made the delicate work even more dangerous.

When you found one mine you always took it for granted that there were more. We knew that the Germans would sometimes set the mines up in a series. They had a kind of black cotton thread that would go from one mine to the next. We would mark out where we had gone and where we had searched so that we could open up a path for the infantry and tanks to get through.

So many times we would bypass or criss-cross the roads and go off into the countryside taking into account the Germans would have mined that particular area. However, the Germans knew what they were doing; they were used to this, and we lost a hell of a lot of vehicles and men getting off those highways. You see— if there were mines on the highway you can bet there were mines on both sides of it as well. In other words, if you wanted to get off the road to avoid mines, you would be going right into another minefield.

Sometimes when there wasn't any immediate fire from the Germans, our tank operators would open up their flap because they needed to look around or perhaps they just wanted to get some fresh air. If the vehicle hit a mine, their head would be gone. I saw this happen too many times and it is an experience that I have never gotten over—I still have nightmares about sights like this.

Besides those damn teller mines they also had other explosives, which were like a big jar but with three prongs sticking out. They were S mines but we called them

Bouncing Bettys—the British called them De-Bollockers. If you hit one of those prongs, it would activate the mine, which would jump out of the ground, around two or three bloody feet, and spray you with shrapnel. If you stepped on one, you didn't have much of a decision to make; if you took your foot off and tried to lie down you would be dead. You couldn't reach down or put anything under the foot because as soon as you let the pressure off it would explode.

I vividly remember the first time I saw this happen. One fella, an infantry boy, stepped on one. He was so young, just like we all were. He knew he was a goner, so he just yelled to his buddies to warn them. When they were clear, he lifted his foot and died; it just tore him apart. In doing so he saved the lives of all the combat personnel around him. He was a hero.

Sometimes we would walk into the middle of a damn minefield and not even realise it. We hadn't set any charges off but there we were, you could see a bit of black thread or steel, so you would shout out, 'Minefield,' and again, 'Minefield,' so people around you would know what was going on. Everybody would just stand still until we figured out what the hell the situation was. Then we just worked on them. We wouldn't take out all the mines, just clear a pathway through and identify it with whatever we had. After we had cleared a path we had to walk in front of the tanks to guide them through safely.

In reality, we were running into minefields from the beaches all the way through and often it was a combination of fatality and wounding that alerted us.

Our progress was slowed at other times by burnt-out and abandoned vehicles blocking the way. They were more than likely booby-trapped so we had to approach them with a lot of caution. Sometimes we would come across three or four burnt-out trucks that had been booby-trapped and were full of explosives. When that happened, we would blow the whole bloody thing up.

*

The Germans tried to slow us up any way they could and a favourite way was to blow the bridges they left behind. They were quite good at dismantling bridges but there were times when we caught them doing it. When that happened, they didn't get away: we killed them.

Being engineers Trix, The Greek and I then had to go underneath a bridge and dismantle the charges that were under there. It didn't happen a lot but it happened enough. Those explosives were tricky and, of course, they were German, and we weren't used to all their techniques and so we had to move very slowly and figure it all out. It was nerve-wracking and it called for a lot of self-control. Keep in mind—while we were under a bridge like that there was a lot going on, usually small arms fire. The enemy would sometimes be watching, knowing that they hadn't had a chance to blow the bridge and they wanted to make sure that we got hurt in some way. We lived under almost constant stress, and to relieve it, we played tricks on each other, no matter what the situation was. I was under a bridge once, reaching up with both hands to remove explosives the Germans had set, and Trix started goosing me with his rifle.

I shouted, 'You sonofabitch, when I get down I'm going to kick the living hell out of you.'

Sometimes a bridge had been blown but there would be sections of it left hanging dangerously so we would complete the job to make it safe. I didn't see it myself, but apparently the column halted at a bridge, as they were not quite sure if it had been rigged to blow or not. There were Germans on the far side and plenty of small-arms fire. Now General Rose pulled up in his jeep and wanted to know why the column had stopped.

One of the infantry guys answered, 'We're not sure if the bridge is safe to cross, Sir.'

Muttering something like, 'Damn it', the general crouched down and made his way across the bridge, ducking a barrage of bullets as he went. He finally stopped to assess the situation, then turned around and came back.

'It's safe,' he said. 'Move out.'

*

Of course, when a bridge had been blown there was no choice but to call up our heavy-duty trucks with the tread-ways and pontoons and get building; as combat engineers, we were putting up those bridges all over northern France and Belgium. I personally didn't work on a lot of them, as my unit tended to spend more time on booby traps and explosives, things like that, but I did work on a few and I can remember the intense resistance we faced while putting them up.

Once there was a bridge across a small river, which had been blown, so we had to stop and rebuild it. We didn't know it, but there were six or seven German tanks hiding in some dense woods to our left. Those Germans were clever, allowing us to get started before opening fire. Our tanks were way back because they couldn't get through. There were three other squads there besides us. Some of them came out of the woods with automatic rifles so we had to let the bridge go for a while. A good few men died. I only escaped by ducking into the icy water. After the fighting died down we regrouped, got back in and finished the job.

We were always pressing forward. Usually we would cover three or four miles a day but now and then we would do around fifty miles; you are talking from very early in the morning to very late at night. Once we moved a hundred miles in one day, which was unheard of. I remember thinking, 'Good God, where the hell are we going?'

Sometimes, especially in France, you would have refugees clogging the roads up; there would be thousands of them either side of the highway. Usually they would have little handcarts piled high with their belongings, trying to get away from whatever town or city was coming under attack. When they saw us coming they used to lie down and let us go on through.

At other times we would encounter pockets of resistance in a village or town, where we slowed up and had to engage in house to house fighting; that was pretty nasty. In all honesty, one village was much like the next to us. We didn't speak the language but what we did understand was the misery and slaughter of the villagers in the places we were going through, caught up in the American and German battle as we moved forward trying to get deeper and deeper into France.

The French Resistance was often able to help us with intelligence. We had boys from Louisiana, down south, who spoke French and could get a lot of information about what was going on. Sometimes the Resistance inadvertently got in our way, which was unfortunate but those times were few and far between. By and large the French Resistance, and the Belgium Resistance, were very helpful. They shared current information, where the Germans were, how many tanks they had, and all that kind of stuff. The Free French would also bring us prisoners who we could interrogate to find out what was going on. They also did a remarkable job in blowing things up and knocking out roadblocks before these could hurt us in any way.

When we took a town there were times when Sergeant Foster told us to halt and we wouldn't go any further. We would make ourselves at ease, so to speak, in a farmhouse or what have you. We had a chance to eat and boil some water for a hot cup of Java; sometimes we would even be able to take a bath if we were lucky enough. At times, we would spend most of the night there but we usually didn't get much sleep.

Despite all the misery and destruction, once we had taken an objective, the locals would be extremely grateful. In France, villagers would gather around and shake our hands and give us flowers, kiss us on the cheeks. They carried wine, which they would try to persuade us to take. We didn't speak any French but some of them knew enough English to express their gratitude for bringing them freedom from the German occupation of their country. Many of them were close to tears.

They would shout, 'Viva America,' with real gusto.

They were quite vocal and demonstrative with their feelings. They would have little American flags that they had made to show their appreciation. We gave the children chocolate and cheese from our rations and the kids loved it.

When cattle got killed on the farms where we were fighting they were butchered by the starving civilians immediately afterwards. They also did the same to the horses; the French had no problem eating horsemeat. They were hungry because of the way the situation was, you see. The war, with its on-going fighting, had destroyed most of the crops and their food supplies. We gave them what we had because we could always get more from our supply people. They were most grateful to get what little food we could give them.

It was a good feeling to be made welcome and to be able to help in some small way but we had to be very careful in these situations because the snipers would take advantage of that type of thing; they were still active in these villages and towns as we were passing through. There weren't a hell of a lot of snipers but the ones that were there, usually up in tall buildings, were taken care of by the infantry.

If someone pointed out a sniper I would grab my M1 rifle and take a look. If I could see the sonofabitch he was dead because my firing was excellent—I had won medals for my marksmanship on the firing range back in Fort Leonard Wood, Missouri.

I remember once we arrived in a small town—like most places the name beats me these days—riding in the half-track and someone yelled 'Sniper.'

I was standing in the well of the half-track by my .50 calibre machine gun. I got down and Sharp, the driver, pulled over to one side but we still couldn't see him. I did the old trick and put my helmet on the end of my rifle and held it up and he shot a hole in the sonofabitch.

I opened up the door on my side of the half-track with my M1 rifle and stayed as close to the door as I could while Sharp gave him a burst from the other side. I gradually got my head in a position where I could see the top of the bombed-out office block and I saw him fire once again; that's all I needed. I trained my M1 on that spot, saw the sonofabitch move and I nailed the bastard. Keep in mind we were young, we had good eyesight, we were physically agile and we were toughened up because of combat. I didn't feel any remorse; after the hedgerows I was used to the cold-blooded nature of war and, besides, he had probably taken out quite a few of our guys, but now he wouldn't hurt anyone any more.

*

People in the towns and villages we liberated had been under such dominance from the Germans—what those soldiers did to some of these people is unthinkable—and, not surprisingly, I did see some retribution being handed out to Nazi collaborators or sympathisers. When the tables had been turned, mob justice was dished out. The guys, of course, were just killed and left to hang but they took it out on the women and shaved their hair off and they would beat them too. We tried to put a stop to things like that because there are other ways of handling it. Part of our job was to take such women, or girls, back into the relative safety of the army. They would talk to them to find out what they knew about the Germans, often providing very useful and timely information.

Fortunately, coming up behind the infantry, we had teams of experienced military people in place that could help set up local governments. They would work with the people who were in that village or town so they could stabilise the situation. Also, there was a lot of intelligence being gathered because the war criminals were going to be brought to justice.

*

On the rare occasions when we had the chance to rest up, the elders of the town, somebody like the mayor, would often come up to us and show us where minefields were. They were fully knowledgeable of their location because before we got there they had been told to be careful around them.

Then the villagers would beg us to help clear the mines and so once again we would make a safe pathway, well marked on both sides, through the mines and re-alert the citizens that there were minefields there. It was especially important to get it through to the children that these were dangerous areas to be in. I saw this with my own eyes on a few occasions where civilians were blown up in a minefield. In one case there was a man and a child who had been blown pretty much to pieces; it's sickening to witness what an anti-personnel mine can do.

Also people would come up and point to their house and say 'Boom boom,' indicating that there may be booby traps. Being engineers, of course, we had to go and take a look at it. Mines in buildings were very cleverly hidden and very cleverly hooked up; they did quite a bit of damage. Once again, they would often be wired up in a string and if one went off the other explosive devices would be triggered as well. Even though we were supposed to be at rest, so to speak, we still had those types of things to do; we were never really out of danger.

*

It had taken us just eighteen days to blaze our way across Northern France, with fighting going on all the time. They were not necessarily big battles, although as we entered September 1944 and crossed the Belgian border, all that was about to change.

Word came through to General Rose that we were to turn ninety degrees and head towards Mons to try and intercept the German 7th Army and other elements, including SS parachutists, to prevent them from getting back to Germany.

History says there were around thirty thousand Germans heading to the area in and around that city. For once we set up roadblocks of our own on all roads leading through the area heading to the German border. Somehow we had managed to surprise the Germans and they walked into an ambush; as a force in full retreat they had no idea we had taken the city.

I can remember my squad engaged alongside the infantry—it was intense, it was fierce, we didn't know that it was going to be that bad. Once again Spearhead had been surrounded by the Germans and there was no front line as such, just combat going on all over the place. We were more on the outskirts of Mons than in the city per se. The engagement lasted for days.

Those Piper Cubs spotted the approaching enemy columns, which appeared to be miles in length, then Thunderbolts were called in and they went to work with bombs and strafing attacks. We also destroyed much of the enemy's transportation at Mons—I believe over a thousand German vehicles were accounted for, clogging the roads as the Germans tried to escape. Once again the towns and villages were full of burnt-out tanks and trucks, dead civilians and cattle. It was a terrible sight, especially seeing the dead children; that really got to us guys.

I saw a couple of situations where our aircraft spotted a train and they went in and bombed the tracks, immobilising the train and then machine-gunning the carriages. They would also alert US troops on the ground so we could mop up.

For one reason or other the battle of Mons never got a big write-up in the history books but it was a major victory for the Allies, as it dealt a terminal blow to the German 7th Army. Already weakened by its losses at the

Falaise Gap, at Mons we further reduced a once mighty army to tatters—Spearhead alone captured nearly ten thousand enemy soldiers at Mons and killed around five thousand more.

The result meant the Germans were in chaos and had been severely weakened—something that would greatly affect their ability to defend their precious Fatherland in the near future.

*

After we left Mons we headed towards Namur—it was a fair sized city and I remember the name because it sounded like the French word for love, amour. A bridge went up there but it wasn't my platoon that built it, I think it was 2nd platoon; we were acting as infantry and helped hold the bridge crossing until they got the job done. The Germans were trying to stop what we had to do but there was no stopping Spearhead.

When Namur finally fell the population came out in the thousands to greet us. Once more, the welcome and flag waving was overwhelming. The people were very pleased to see us indeed; they all had smiles on their faces. The girls would come up and put their arms around you and give you a big hug; they were quite liberal in terms of kissing you and making you feel like a victorious soldier. They had flowers, sandwiches and cake—where they had got these luxuries from I don't know.

We were literally smothered by the welcome of the Belgian people. They would put their arms around us and they didn't want us to move on.

'You have got to stay here,' they would say. 'The Germans might come back.'

'They won't,' we assured them. Of course, we had no way of knowing at that time that the Battle of the Bulge would change everything for them.

They invited us into their homes, but of course we couldn't go because we were only passing through. When Sergeant Foster gave the order to move out, we moved there and then, not five minutes later, not tomorrow morning, but now.

On very rare occasions, we would share a victory drink. Our officers wouldn't tolerate any heavy drinking but would turn a blind eye to one or two glasses of beer. To be honest with you, none of the guys in my squad were heavy drinkers; they were good soldiers and very dedicated. We also knew that danger was never very far away and we had to stay alert to stay alive.

Then, early in the second week of September 1944, we moved on to a full frontal attack on Liège, which is close to the German border. The intensity from the German Army increased considerably because they knew that the next stop, for the Allied troops, was their homeland. We lost a hell of a lot of guys taking Liège. The terrain had changed from wide plains to hill country, with narrow roads and woods, which made it ideal for holding warfare. The one thing that stands out in the memory with Liège, as was the case with Namur, were the countless roadblocks, where they had set up a piece of artillery and three or four tanks to stop us getting through. We seldom saw those guns; they were so well camouflaged and well defended. There would also be a hell of a lot of infantry guarding those guns. They were well dug in. And not only that, they had put in landmines surrounding those gun emplacements. They intended to have a battle and stop us and those roadblocks took out quite a number of our tanks.

Roadblocks were usually so well defended it might take four or five days to take them out. Sometimes we had to withdraw and let our artillery do its job in order to move forwards.

I can remember setting up various situations where we could keep an eye on what the Germans were doing. We also set up roadblocks of our own to make sure that they weren't going to come back through. Maybe three or four tanks would break loose and try to get through but we would have an anti-tank gun set up to put paid to that.

We removed countless roadblocks in and around the various towns, where many Germans manning them got killed. Others were wounded and in pretty bad shape but there was not much that we could do to help them. Our medics on the other hand, who were following us really close, did what they could for the German casualties. First and foremost they took care of the American casualties and then they were gentle and kind in helping the Germans who had got wounded. Some of them were dying and nothing could be done for them.

*

Just outside Liège was a castle, or chateau as they called them; it wasn't enormous but it was big and it even had a ditch around it that looked as though it had once been a moat. We were looking for possible Germans hiding out near there when the owner approached us.

After the handshakes and the hugs and all that kind of stuff he invited us into his castle, which was enormous inside and so clean. His wife and family were in there, and they spoke some English. Our host was an old gentleman and so grateful that he showered us in champagne that we had to kindly decline. We still had to secure the castle and make sure it was safe before anyone could relax. He then took us outside. The grounds had beautiful flowers and gardens. He showed us where he had buried his collection of antique guns, along with a lot of silver and some gold. He didn't want the Germans getting their hands on them. I don't think he was nobility, I think that he was an industrialist who had bought the castle and made it his home, until the Germans had arrived and kicked him out. They were so happy to get rid of them; they were also happy that the

Germans hadn't wrecked the place when they left. After helping the owner and his family, we managed some rest and recuperation and had some sleep. We knew that there would be no interference from the enemy because we had driven them back, so we just plain relaxed there for three or four hours. We just enjoyed the ability to sit down and take it easy and have a little bit of food. Then the owner asked us to sweep the place for any mines before we left, which we were happy to do. Luckily we didn't find any.

*

Just outside of Liège we came to a halt and were told to check our ammunition and our water canteens because we were going to be in for quite a show. Even then I didn't really know that we were actually preparing for the assault on Germany itself; we were regrouping because the Siegfried Line was coming up.

Chapter 10

Crossing the Siegfried Line

When a nation has thought as long and hard about all-out war as Germany had, you can bet that it had done its homework. That sure was evident when we came face to face with the Siegfried Line.

The Germans knew that one day they may need to batten down their hatches, as it were, so they built that line. In all fairness it was a mighty impressive system of defences, stretching along the whole German western frontier for almost four hundred miles, from Holland to Switzerland. It wasn't just one line of defence; in some areas it was a mile deep, involving forts, tunnels, pillboxes, minefields, antitank ditches and dragon's teeth, which were pyramid blocks made out of reinforced concrete that easily stopped our tanks.

That damned border defence had first been built for the Great War but had been hugely extended and improved by the time we tried to smash our way through. They even constructed what looked like small villages but turned out to be fortified homes made out of thick concrete. Even the German pillboxes, which looked haphazardly placed, were well thought out and covered each other—the whole thing was a master-class in defensive warfare.

In the second week of September 1944 I saw it for myself. I knew then that we had reached the border because I had read about the Siegfried Line in the British newspapers. Before that I didn't know where we were, as I have said; one country looked like any other to us guys. I think our tanker drivers had a map that they could refer to but the average GI just didn't realise, until we saw that line, that by God this was Germany.

I knew that breaking through wasn't going to be an easy task. I turned to Trix and said, 'This is a heads up ball game now because these people are really going to put on one hell of a show defending their country.'

I felt quite alarmed, to be honest, because I had the inclination that if somebody was coming into my country, I would fight to the death. I always admired the tenacity of the German soldier; they were literally fighting for their country. I didn't have any sympathy for them but I admired the skill and determination that these guys were showing. They would take unusual chances to try and hold the line but they were fighting a losing battle because for every one of our tanks they took out we were able to put two back in. If they put ten men on the line we would put twenty and they knew this. The overwhelming capacity of the United States,

Canada, Great Britain and our other Allies to put these forces into play was decisive.

*

When it came to getting across the line my squad was giving fire support for the guys who were going to blow up the dragon's teeth. I was on my .50 calibre up on the half-track and the gun got so hot it quit on me a couple of times so I had to reach down for my rifle, which I kept by my feet, until it cooled off. It was very dangerous being in the turret because it made me an easy target. I could actually feel live ammo whooshing right past my ears. It scared the shit out of me, I can tell you, and to this day I can still remember it vividly.

Although at this point I wasn't directly involved in the explosive work, I saw it happening, and it took a considerable amount of effort to smash our way through. The teeth stood about three-and-a-half feet above the ground and were solid reinforced concrete. They were buried deep into the ground. There were miles of them, and it took several days to break through. In the process we lost many of our guys; some were killed, a lot more were wounded.

We were briefed that the Siegfried Line was full of mines, and we had to be extremely careful. Fortunately when they were blowing up the dragon's teeth they blew up a lot of mines as well, but before the dragon's teeth there were minefields and after the dragon's teeth there were minefields; all over the place.

My platoon was also tasked with searching and feeling the ground for mines and making a path so the tanks, half-tracks, jeeps and two-and-a-half-tonne trucks could get through without being blown up. By then we did have some electronic metal detectors but most of the time it meant getting on your hands and knees, with your dagger, and feeling around in the earth or snow real gently. Most times the Germans would be firing at you while you were doing this. I was keenly aware, during that particular time of my life as a soldier, that my life was really on the line.

*

The Siegfried Line wasn't something that was taken lightly. A lot of lives were lost crossing it, but cross it we eventually did. We were the first Allied troops to set foot on German soil but, at the time, we didn't know that.

We had broken through east of Aachen—a fairly large city entrenched in German history, and not far from another city, Stolberg. For a while there were no German troops, they had gone, it was just civilians. There were very few people on the streets so we just held our position tight on the outskirts of Aachen.

Part of our job, as always, was clearing things out so

we went into homes and office buildings to make sure that things were really clear. Going in we were always mindful to check to see if there were any booby traps. We would most commonly find them on doors or stairs. They used a length of wire or cord attached to a detonator in explosives so when you opened the door, or tripped the wire on the stairs, it would blow. They also used pressure detonators that they would place under the stair tread or carpet; we would stand back and throw something on it to set it off, they were so sensitive. It was a damn sight safer than trying to defuse it.

You wouldn't just open a door—you would kick the sonofabitch in and immediately fall to the floor. Or you would shoot around the lock until it was shattered and it fell to the floor, then you knew there was nothing on the other side to be concerned about because you had blasted it away. If there was a booby-trap it would blow but you would be safely backed out the way.

One time I busted into this big office building with my buddies. I went off to the right and went into this room, very, very cautiously because you never knew what the hell was on the other side of the door, and there was a man sat at a desk who had committed suicide.

We ran into suicides with some frequency when we got into Germany when we were moving into buildings searching for the Germans. Another time I went in and there was a man, woman and about three or four children who had all committed suicide. I heard similar stories from the other guys as well, that people had done foolish things because they thought that the Americans were going to hurt them. At the time it was hard to take—it was so very sad and such a waste of life.

After the war I asked some Germans why they did that and they said that they had been told that the Americans were going to rape and kill them and steal their stuff. I asked if they had also got that information about the British and they said yes, they were told that too. They said that they had been quite surprised when that didn't happen.

*

The fighting was intense. We were moving into their own backyard so to speak, and they didn't like it one bit. There was a lot of killing on our part and certainly the Germans were trying to inflict as much damage on us as they could. The resistance became stronger and stronger as we advanced further into Germany.

We drove their Army out of towns and cities through street-to-street fighting. It was bloody and it was a scary situation because we couldn't trust the civilians like we could in France and Belgium. Not that we were nasty to them but keep in mind that some of the soldiers put on civilian clothes; we were told to be careful of that.

People were trying to get out of the towns and cities but not to the extent that we witnessed in Belgium and

France. There was a constant trickle of them coming out. They knew that we were occupying their country and as you can imagine, they were none too happy about it and they sure showed it. There was a mixture of insolence and fear but some were genuinely glad to see the Americans. There were others who had just given up, the country wasn't theirs anymore and there was a look of despair on their faces. We treated them like we treated any other civilians, with respect and caution.

The people there were obviously very scared so we had to try and introduce the idea that we were not villains. It took a considerable sustained effort to reassure them that we were after the German Army, not the civilians.

People had tried to barricade themselves into their homes. We had to go into some of those homes, especially the ones that showed some resistance with small arms fire. When we finally got in, we usually found quite a few dead soldiers. Others had their hands in the air ready to give up and there were sometimes civilians who lived there who had also gotten killed. Sometimes there were children too. That's what war is sometimes like, you try to take the enemy and sometimes they use civilians for protection. We killed a lot of people. Unfortunately, some of them were civilians.

It's hard for me to describe, at this time of my life, the amount of bloodshed and mayhem that existed once we had crossed over into Germany. The men in uniform didn't give me a problem when I saw them dead but when I saw civilians being wounded or killed that didn't settle well with me at all. Certainly we felt it when we saw that children had gotten injured or killed. Then again, the German soldiers in these homes also have to share the responsibility.

There were so many of these bed sheets to show signs of surrender, hanging out of windows, and the civilians trying to recognise the hopelessness of the situation. They would shout out in German various things that we couldn't understand but the gist of it was they were non-combatant and wanted to give up. Some had their little white flags to show that they weren't combatants.

In small towns and villages, sometimes the Germans would come out with those printed messages on red sheets of paper that had been dropped by our aircraft, which stated in both German and English that they wanted to surrender.

There were times when these Hitler Youths would tie themselves up in a big tree. They were only around fifteen or sixteen, just kids, and they would watch us coming through and have a go at us. They were staunch believers in Adolf Hitler and his regime and they were putting their lives on the line right smack in front of us. Now, trying to take out a young boy up in a tree shooting at you wasn't an easy thing to do but it had to be done. We tried our best not to kill them and looked to shoot them in the leg or something, just to get them to stop, but they were fanatics. We became more aware after the first couple of times this happened.

When we were fighting in the towns and villages we would get out of the half-track or, if we had been riding on the back of a tank, we would get off, and go around to the front and walk in the street to find out what was going on. You had to be very careful when you went around a corner because way up that street might be a German tank or anti-tank gun staring right back at you. Usually we ran into a barrage of small arms fire.

Getting around was not easy and often the streets would be filled with rubble and it would be very difficult to run across. If there was considerable incoming mail and someone had to cross the street, then we would give them some cover fire. When one of the guys would run across you would not look at him. You would be looking around for any sign of movement in case a German is out there checking you. Normally we would try to take out that opposition before the guy would try to cross the street, but we couldn't always do that, so there would be fatalities or serious injuries.

We had to be ever watchful of young children and civilians getting in our line of fire. At times that would be to our detriment, with one of us either missing a shot or getting hurt because we were taking care to look before we used our weapons. People would often go into their cellars so you had to be careful when you were house-to-house fighting. We tried our best not to kill or injure the civilians but because of the severity of combat at times it was unavoidable. Those memories are hard to live with.

At times, in moving through the streets, we would see a German tank and we would look back at our tank and make that T sign and point out where it was. The value of that was immeasurable for the tanker because they were looking through a slit that was very thin and not very wide and the amount of information they got looking through that slit was very limited.

If we saw a tank we would normally stay where we were and get as much protection as we could from a building or vehicle, you name it, and wait to see what our tank was going to do. We would get out of its way. Sometimes it would go through the damn building, literally. The tank commander would know what to do once we had pointed out the German tank. Our tankers were fearless. With the limited information we gave them, they used it to their best advantage. It saved many of our tanks and the lives of our tankers. We couldn't do it often because there was so much going on but we did the best we could under the circumstances. The German infantry also had a weapon similar to a bazooka and they were very effective, especially at short range. They were built for close combat, about the same size as our bazookas and to be honest, a rocket is a rocket—once it hits it does considerable damage.

*

When we came across a situation like a row or terrace of houses or a big apartment block, one of the things that we used to do was work our way up to the top floor. That in itself was kind of dicey because the Germans were often waiting for us; we lost a lot of guys doing that. Normally it would be a squad of infantry taking the lead and with them would be a couple of combat engineers with explosives that we always carried on us. Then, when they reached the top they would call for an engineer and we would blast a hole in the bloody wall because it's a damn sight easier fighting your way downstairs than trying to fight upstairs with them looking down on you. Afterwards you could go up to the top floor and look clear through where we blasted our holes.

We used plastic explosives, Composition C, which was just like putty. You could throw that stuff around and it wouldn't go off. It wasn't unstable like dynamite, which I hated. We would put the detonator in, which was about the size of your little finger, and then we would ignite the fuse and back the hell out of the way. Once we were set up we would shout, 'We are going to blow.' The guys would take shelter behind a wall or on the stairs; we would count it down, and wait for the explosion.

After I blew the hole in the wall, I would back off and let the infantry get in to do their job. We had to keep moving; if you didn't kill the Germans, they would kill you. It was that simple. As the infantry moved through the opening, they met fierce resistance on every floor, all the way down to the basement. They would be under intense fire, including hand grenades.

We used that technique a number of times, which was very useful. The Germans eventually learned to recognise it, and cleared out when we started. That certainly saved a lot of our boys' lives.

Much of the time, we would work alongside the infantry to go into wherever the Germans were, to feel out what the situation was and give feedback to command. At times I went out with a squad at night to try and capture some so that our intelligence guys could talk to them and find out what was going on. Whenever we did go out at night we had to be very careful because we would sometimes stumble into the Germans and all hell would break loose.

When this happened, we would have to go in there and shake them up. During a lot of exchanges you would be using grenades because you were into close combat. As a result, most times when we took our captured Germans back they were wounded. There weren't many times when we were able to take back what we called 'a whole German'.

I do remember on one occasion we lost Trix on a night patrol. He was clearing some mines from the road that were loaded with trip wires when he heard the sound of vehicles advancing. Recognising these as Germans he quickly placed some of the mines in a patch of the road that the Germans would believe to be clear and rigged a trip wire to them then hid nearby. When the vehicles hit the mine, they exploded.

Thank God he had the good sense to stay well hidden until it was daylight and safe to move.

*

After the fighting died down we were just sat there holding the line. There were still exchanges of artillery; they were still lobbing them in as we used to say, but the intensity was less severe.

I was on a machine gun with Trix and The Greek one time when someone hollered, 'Hey Limey, you're going to Paris.'

I turned to Trix and said, 'He's kidding' before shouting, 'Bugger off.'

But it was Sergeant Foster and he said, 'Your name was pulled out of the hat and you have three days in Paris.'

Occasionally, there were a few days' R&R available, and obviously we couldn't all go, so they put all our names in a helmet and drew one. If your name came up, you were one lucky sonofabitch. That day, it was my turn to be lucky.

I looked at Trix and said, 'I'll see ya, I'm going to Paris.'

He said, 'You ain't going you sonofabitch, unless I go along with ya.'

I said, 'You can't, it was just my name pulled out of that hat.'

'You can't go, you haven't got any money,' he said.

'You do,' I said.

'Okay,' he said.

He turned out his pockets; they were full of chewing tobacco, candy wrappers and God knows what, and there was around a hundred dollars.

I picked the money up and put it in my pocket and said, 'I'm off.'

I went down and found Sergeant Foster and asked when we were leaving and he said, 'In about an hour, just sit back.' And so I did.

A break from frontline activity and going into Paris with plenty of food, with a hundred dollars, which was a reasonable amount of money in those days, was a most unusual experience for me.

I went down in a two-and-a-half-tonne truck and was dropped off, near the Opera House in Paris, at this posh hotel where they housed us GIs. I went in that hotel room and took the best damn shower of my life—I had been on the frontline for months and there were no washrooms up there I can tell you; the mud and dirt was caked on.

I had some clean socks and underwear to put on before wearing my class A uniform. I stood in front of the mirror and placed my cap on my head and said, 'By God you look good, Limey. I'm ready for Paris.' Then I stepped out onto the streets of the city and, with the help of one of the many US jeeps that were moving around, took in all the mighty fine sights, the Eiffel Tower, the Arc de Triomphe, Notre Dame. I had spent many months knee deep in the rubble of flattened buildings yet here I was in the most beautiful city in the world—its amazing architecture had been left untouched by bombs on Hitler's orders—and it sure was quite a sight for a poor Swansea kid.

Later I was walking along this quiet backstreet and this girl was standing outside her door; she was a very pretty French girl, so I said, 'Howdy.'

And she said 'Howdy' back.

We got to talking and her father came to the door and invited me in. It was one of those big apartment blocks that go up several storeys with shutters on the windows and small balconies right at the top in the loft apartments.

The girl was about seventeen, she didn't speak much English and she said 'Vive la France,' and all that kind of stuff. It was nice to go in there and have a good meal with a nice family, there were no under the table thoughts or anything like that; it was just a lovely part of being in Paris for those three days. I was treated like a king.

Later that night I did have a few drinks—it's what The Greek and Trix would have wanted me to do—

then I had one of the best night's sleep of my life. That bed in that posh hotel was bloody fantastic—I really felt like royalty.

The second night I got into a poker game with a bunch of guys and some broads at a nearby hotel. For some reason it ended up being strip poker. I had my shirt off, another guy had his pants off, we were drinking and having one hell of a good time singing and what have you. Although there were women present there was no funny business, it was just a bunch of guys having a good time away from all the killing and bloodshed.

When I woke up the next morning I couldn't find my shirt or my doggone boots but there was a pair of red wooden clogs at the foot of the bed and a hotel dressing gown, which I had to wear till I could locate a shirt. I had had quite a bit to drink and must have blacked out because I still don't remember much. As me and the rest of the guys left, a passing US Army jeep picked us up and took us back to the hotel that was being used as a base for US soldiers. When the military police there saw those red clogs they burst out laughing and then finally sent me to the quartermaster for new boots.

I finally managed to get things together and made my way to the two-and-a-half-tonne truck; only for the sergeant to tell me, 'You're not getting out of here today.'

'Why the hell not?' I asked.

'The last truck left at midday. The next is at eleven

hundred hours tomorrow morning.' When I finally got back to the line I was a day late. One of the guys said, 'The captain wants to see you.'

With a sinking feeling in my gut, I went to his command post and when he saw me he said, 'You know you are twenty-four hours AWOL? It's gone down as a matter of record.'

He added, 'I can have you shot.'

I said. 'Please don't do that sir, I am a damn good soldier and will continue to be. I will make you proud.'

*

At that time I was an acting corporal and had only been one for about a week. He took my stripe away and said, 'I'm going to put you on KP (kitchen police) duty.'

I said, 'You can't, I'm up on the line.'

He just glared at me and said, 'Get out of here, Limey, and don't let it happen again.'

How the hell could I do it again? That was the only break I caught in months on the line. When Trix and The Greek saw me they asked if I had had a good time.

'You doggone betcha,' I replied.

'How were the broads?' asked the Greek.

'Fine.'

'How was the drinking?' asked Trix.

'Fine.'

The Greek asked, 'Did you meet anybody?'

'That would be telling.'

Then Trix got to the point and said, 'Did you bring me any booze back?'

'Don't be so bloody soft,' I replied. If there's one place on God's earth you don't need booze it's the front line.

'So where's my hundred dollars then?' mumbled Trix.

'Don't worry, you'll get it,' I told him.

*

Another pleasant surprise happened a few weeks later as we were holding the line—Thanksgiving. This US holiday was still a relatively new concept to me being a Welsh boy. I first saw it in New York, with my friend Joe Harris and his wife. Families in those days were very large, and they brought out the turkey with all the trimmings; relatives would turn up with a plate of potatoes or carrots or a pie, they all brought a dish and sat around the table to enjoy Thanksgiving dinner. It was an opportunity to have a good meal with friends, family and neighbours.

Well on November 27, 1944, we were all dug in some Godforsaken field, which was fortunately relatively quiet with only the occasional burst of fire, and they gave us turkey dinners. I can still recall it being a bright, cold sunny day with blue skies and heavy frost.

These guys risked their lives—some of them got hurt—to bring us Thanksgiving dinner on the front line. I thought to myself, by God, look at this, it's fantastic. You cannot imagine what it was like for us after so many months of hardship to have that hot meal brought to us.

I also remember that day for another reason. It was the day that I heard my first jet engine. We just looked at each other because we didn't know what the hell it was. This German pilot came in low at a tremendous speed, it was the first jet aeroplane that I had ever seen. I thought it sounded like a bunch of trains backing up, bang, bang, bang. And you felt the vibration. We barely caught sight of it—just saw the tail end of the son of a gun way out yonder. To hear that noise and try to put it all together, that was frightening. Later we got word that it was a jet-propelled German aircraft—we knew then that we had better win this bloody war soon.

*

We were still holding the line into December 1944. My squad were housed temporarily in this big house that we had commandeered. We had got all the Germans out and this was how we kept warm. The European winter was really beginning to bite. You could see a lot of German civilians around. They were getting ready for Weihnachten, Christmas, but there was still plenty of small-arms fire flying around.

As we settled in for the evening Sergeant Foster said

to me, 'Limey, I want you to go to the half-track and get some chewing tobacco for me.' Or it may have been to get his coat because there was heavy snow.

As I got near the half-track I heard a whistling sound fast approaching and I hit the deck. I heard that whistling noise and thought to myself, 'This is it, I'm a goner.' Without any exaggeration that shell passed within about two foot of my head and tore into the bottom of the building behind me, killing some of our boys inside and injuring others. Fortunately, my squad was in the other side of the building and escaped the worst of the impact.

I started to get up and then another one came in; they had zeroed in on us. However, when an artillery piece fires at you it gives its position away too. Our own artillery boys waded in and there was a duel going on. I was caught in the middle of it and felt the concussions and heard it all. I was lying as flat as I could right next to the half-track so I tried to get underneath. I lay there until I thought it safe to move and I crawled back inside the building. Seeing all the damage brought home to me how lucky I had been. Whatever I was supposed to get I didn't get it.

That incident is so vivid in my mind I can still feel it today; sometimes I dream about it. It spelt death; that's what that doggone noise spelt to me—war and death. I didn't know it then but a few days later things were going to get a hell of a lot worse.

Chapter 11

Combat

At times before we moved into a situation in a village or town we would stop and the officers and non-commissioned officers would talk out the plan of attack. This would include our sergeants and lieutenants.

While the officers were having their discussion we were preoccupied with trying to get battle-ready, as we called it. There were things that needed to be done. We had to check that our rifles were clean, that we had enough ammunition, and that we had some water on us and so on. We just checked things the best we could before we moved into these combat situations. We were pretty calm and collected, and personally speaking I usually didn't feel too anxious before going in.

We never knew what to expect, whether there's going to be some sonofabitch ready to cut your throat or put a bullet in you or not. Many of us guys never thought about our own personal safety. Much of the time you're not thinking of losing your life, that's the God's truth, you're thinking of the damage you are going to inflict.

Then, when that order came, you didn't hesitate. Sergeant Foster would say, 'Move.' And that was it.

The best way to describe combat is it's a continuous series of situations where you are coming face-to-face with the enemy and the closer you get, the more intense the fire becomes.

I may not have been scared preparing for whatever we had to do but that changed when I was in the middle of it all. I became very sensitive to everything that was going on because if you didn't you would be dead. When you are in the middle of small arms or machine gunfire your senses are heightened, you are concentrating, you are looking at everything that is going on and continually revaluating everything that is happening all around you.

Sometimes it scared the living crap out of me knowing we were moving into a situation which involved those bloody bazookas, machine gun nests, tanks, those awful 88s and mortar fire, which I hated as it was so unpredictable. Sometimes artillery was also used, inflicting considerable damage on us guys. We also had to contend with those damned snipers in tall buildings, or having to break down a door knowing those bastards were in there.

Although we planned ahead, it was difficult to predict exactly what we were going to face, as each situation was different, and the situation itself controlled everything else. You might have talked about this or that but the unfolding situation controlled whatever the hell you were going to do in the final analysis of battle.

We just played it by ear and hoped to God that we made the right decisions. Religion, for most of us, played a big part in our moving forward; we placed our trust in Almighty God, realising that there was a power greater than ourselves who was going to help us. A lot of Americans felt that way. Keep in mind that most Americans used to go to church every Sunday so religion was a great comfort to us.

*

In the immediate vicinity of a combat situation you would have buildings on fire including people's homes; you would have a lot of death and destruction right there facing you. We would move into these areas and there would be explosions, which the Germans would have set up and set off to try and stop us coming through.

The smoke at times was so bad we just couldn't see; it was so intense. Our objective was to get from this point through all that bloody smoke and take care of whatever situation was out there. We just had to wait and judge when a clear patch would come up and move ahead the best we could; cautiously, because we weren't fools. Sometimes we would have to wait for an hour or two before we could move.

The despair on the faces of civilians in these villages and towns, whether in Germany or places like Liège and Namur, told a story. There was so much bloodshed that

I used to think to myself 'How the hell are we going to get through all of this?' But we did.

The roads would be very effectively blocked with anti-tank guns behind the barriers they had built, not to mention the rubble of collapsed buildings caused by artillery and air bombardment from both sides.

At times we were faced with individual rifle fire and there were times when you would be looking at machine gun fire. When we spotted a machine gun nest our sergeant would say, 'Okay, we are going to take this out.' If we were close enough we would use hand grenades, other than that we used our tommy guns or we would use a bazooka.

Many times we would be surprised; we would be walking along and all of a sudden all hell would break loose. We had to hit the ground and take a look at what was going on. Sometimes the sergeant wasn't there; we just had to move in and do what we had to do and clear the way.

We were a strong team, we had to be to survive and get the job done, but a team consists of individuals and at times you have to make individual decisions. Sometimes, we would have to break off in ones or twos, or a small group, to deal with a particular issue. Foster would see things that we might not see and he would shout out, 'Limey,' or whoever, and he would point and stress that there was something over yonder that you had to look at or be careful of, such as pillboxes.

They were made of such thick concrete and reinforced steel that the guys behind them had the advantage; they were so well protected. Trying to knock out a pillbox was extremely dangerous. If you crawled up close to the sonsofbitches, and they knew you were out there, they would just drop a hand grenade out the opening and duck back down inside for safety.

Many times we would use a Bangalore torpedo. We would try to get it as close to the pillbox as we could, moving quietly, and explode the sonofabitch. The blast would go up past the opening and that would keep their heads down. Straight afterwards we would rush up, as we knew they sure as hell weren't looking out; then we would lob our grenades into the opening and duck back down ourselves.

*

Combat is a very brutal word that, in my estimation, means destroy. When you join the American Army you have to learn and adhere to standing orders and the one that I remember most is, 'When you enter into combat you seek and destroy the enemy.'

In terms of killing, I injured or killed a fair number of German soldiers, from the beaches all the way through, including in Germany.

When you first get into combat and start killing people, I felt this is my duty, this is what I was told to do, get out there and kill the enemy; and although it was hard, that's what I did. When I saw my buddies around me getting killed and losing parts of their bodies I thought this now is in return for what they are doing to us. We are inflicting upon them the damage that they are trying to inflict upon us. You are wearing the uniform of your country and this is what you have got to do; you have got to kill the enemy. This is the way that it settled with me.

As far as the actual physical moment of taking a life, I don't think that I felt anything; I would call it numbness. It was a situation where you would look at a uniform, that's the way I put it into my head, this is what I'm supposed to do, I'm a soldier and we're at war. That's the kind of rationalisation that was absolutely necessary to do the job I had to do.

*

Almost every time you went into a combat situation you were witnessing friends of yours, or guys you had spoken to, getting killed right next to you. Obviously, I didn't know every single one of them well but most of them I had bumped into and spoken to. You may stand next to each other very briefly, waiting to go into a situation, then move out, and they would be killed. There were a number of instances where guys died in front of me as we were into street fighting or out in open fields and a guy would get hit and I would be next to him.

Once, I think it was Aachen, we were going through, as usual, a hell of a lot of intense fire when this guy on my right wanted to take a look over the pile of rubble we were sheltering behind. When he poked his head up, they blew most of it away. I saw that on many occasions; it's something that stays with you all your life. It was bad enough looking at the Germans when they had lost parts of their bodies but when it comes to your buddies we were a band of brothers, there's no doubting that. If a man got hurt, we all got hurt, that's the way it was.

What it did to me, and I think that I talk for a lot of the guys, was made me determined, by God, to make that life count. You were determined to make sure that this man, who had lost his life, didn't lose it for nothing. It reaffirmed for me that I was going to get through this war and kill a lot of these sonsofbitches until it ended. To me it was a very deep commitment to my buddies who I had been with since the beaches. I took it to heart. You do form a very close relationship with the guys around you. They are more than brothers because these guys had helped save your life, as well as you helping to save theirs, and, when a guy went down, I felt it for sure.

As they were dying they would talk about their families, especially their mothers; that's what they wanted to talk about. I found it most unusual, but, you see, my family life and that of these guys were totally different; I left home when I was fifteen and I didn't have that close family attachment. But here were these guys saying,

'Make sure that my mother knows about this.' And I would say, 'Yes, you betcha.'

There wasn't much I could do from a practical point of view.

As I have said before, you are told to leave it to the medics but that was something that was pretty hard for me to do, to back off, because I wanted to know if the guy was going to make it. But you had to keep moving most times because the activity from the enemy around you was constant. That's the word, constant: time and time again we were in those street fights, in houses, at times crawling along and running into damn rats and animals that had been gutted and killed, the stench was awful.

I remember one young fella in particular, he had a wound in his gut and he was bleeding pretty badly. He said to me, 'I ain't going to make it.'

I said, 'Let's just wait and see.' I was hollering for the medic.

I asked this guy, 'Where are you from?'

He said, 'Tennessee.' The way he was talking he sounded like he was a mountain boy; they have a particular drawl when they talk, which I liked.

We talked for a while. He was telling me about his family, his mom, and when he was a young boy. He was still young, about my age, nineteen or twenty. Then the medic arrived and I handed him over. I knew he was dying; he didn't make it. Those kind of things happened when you made your way through combat.

In the middle of it all you would find quite a few chaplains. Now they weren't that young, they had quite a bit of age on them; from my perspective they were old men of thirty. These men would pay no attention to the array of firepower and the threat that was coming in from the Germans when they were kneeling down with a man who was dying. I saw this on quite a number of occasions. They would hold the man's hand and make the sign of the Cross and say a few words. That was something that always touched me, to see a man without a rifle, who was there as a Christian, risk his life to bring comfort to others. If he were of another faith, the chaplain would accommodate that. When they died, as too many did, the padre would try and leave the body in a respectable position and, if he could, he would cover the face, and give respect to the death of that particular soldier.

*

On a few occasions we had a journalist with us; not all the time but occasionally they would turn up. They also did not pay particular attention to their own lives. They would be out there, when all hell was breaking loose, standing taking pictures. They weren't just reporters from the big papers, like the *Washington Post* or *New York Times*, but also from the smaller cities. They would be moving along with the guys, trying to make the opportunity to talk to some of them, trying to get stories and taking pictures; in a sense they were fearless like the chaplains. They wanted to find out what was happening to the American GI up on the line to report it back to Chicago, New York, Los Angeles or wherever. They wanted to paint a picture of what was going on. I admired that immensely because they were getting word back to families in the United States of where the hell we were at and what we were doing.

*

After it was all over and I looked around and saw the devastation, the bloodshed and bodies of friends and comrades, I would often get a feeling of hopelessness.

All in all, as anyone who has been in combat will tell you, the sights, sounds and smells of the aftermath of combat are horrendous, especially in civilian areas and farms. There are bodies of soldiers, non-soldiers, women and, worst of all, children. They are just lying right there where they had been killed or wounded. Animals too—we are talking scores of animals, horses, cattle, cats and dogs. We just didn't know how to react; nothing prepares you for such sights.

'What in the hell am I into here?' I asked myself, 'Where's this all leading?'

It was questions like that, the hopelessness, the horror on both sides, to get to this advantage point that we had been ordered to take, that sometimes got inside your head.

I saw people crying outside their homes, looks of hopelessness on their faces, hugging each other amidst wails of anguish and despair, trying to comfort their children and each other. I saw people holding their dead loved ones, some of whom were wounded themselves. All around was smoke and flames, broken buildings, streets piled with rubble and vehicles burning. You take any battlefield and this is what you find when things die down.

Too often I saw the devastation of what the German Army and we had done to whole villages or towns, destroying the communities, the people, the buildings. And I still remember and experience the hopelessness to this day.

*

After each situation a special detail, graves registration, would come around and attend to the fallen soldiers. They knew how to deal with and remove the bodies with compassion and respect because this man had just given his life for his country.

When they arrived they would look for the dog tags we all wore—they had your serial number on them—to identify the body. At times you would see a rifle with its bayonet stuck in the ground upside down and the guy's dog tags would be on the butt of the rifle. They would move the bodies to a respectful resting place before they were buried locally in the special cemeteries established over there.

It was an important job because it carried respect for the bodies of the fallen soldiers on both sides. They were not left to lay around exposed to the ravages of nature. The way these guys handled them, the gentleness and the care, you could almost feel it coming off them. I couldn't do it myself. There must be something special about their character to do that job; they were so gentle and so understanding. When they picked up that body it was with great respect.

On occasion, we would come across a few guys just lying there and I didn't like the thought that somebody's son was left there like that and might have been overlooked, so I took the time to slap their bayonet to their rifle and slam it into the ground as hard as I could, put his helmet and dog tags on it before saying a quick prayer and moving on. I saw much of that kind of thing in my five campaigns.

As guys we looked on the aftermath in silence. We didn't talk about it amongst ourselves. One of the reasons for that was it was so heavy, and so much had gone down, that talking wouldn't have done anything at all.

Feelings are a different thing. There were plenty of feelings from the GIs who had been through these combat situations. Guys would be sitting down smoking a cigarette and shaking their heads, some of them close to tears—especially if one of our own boys had gotten killed. Others would just walk off a couple of hundred yards from the main group to be by themselves.

We didn't really try to articulate what we were feeling. Sometimes we would say, 'Well the bastards asked for it and, by God, they got it.'

Bottling it up was to be pretty much the pattern for the rest of our lives; certainly mine.

*

But also, as is human nature, when you had taken a particular town or village there was a kind of relief. You certainly looked around, as far as your platoon is concerned, for familiar faces. I always assumed that Trix and The Greek were okay. There were times in a big city where I would look around for them because I may have been assigned to another squad or platoon. There would be considerable relief when I saw that the guys were okay.

Sergeant Foster would take stock of things after a particular objective had been achieved and write a report on who was alive, wounded and killed. If the situation was right, when the fighting had died down, we would get together and the padre would hold a service. You might get twenty or so guys in attendance. I went to quite a few and found them comforting to realise that I wasn't alone.

There was also a huge relief following combat as it meant we could get into one of the abandoned homes and stretch out for an hour or so. We would sit around and talk while we were waiting for further commands. We would talk about home, family and friends; keep in mind we were young guys so we had a lot of sweethearts and girlfriends, to gas about. Usually it was about what you were going to do when you got back to civilian life, what you were going to do with your life, where you were going to go, that kind of thing. There were only a few married older guys, they would talk about their wives and a few had young children. You could see when they were talking how they really missed their families.

Sometimes one of the guys would say, 'Hey Limey, tell us about Wales.' They were interested in hearing about the difference between the English, Irish, Welsh and the Scots. I used to explain to them that the Welsh had their own language and a separate identity. The guys loved hearing about it, and it took their minds off the horrors of war for a little while.

There were at other times moments of humour which were a release from the anxiety and tension that was felt by us guys sitting there waiting to go into a combat situation or getting out of it. Sometimes, right in the middle of combat, there would be various moments of humour.

The humour would come out in subtle ways. Sometimes the guys would deliberately break wind in the foxhole right next to you. 'It's those army beans again,' they would laugh.

I remember a time once when Trix, The Greek and I were clearing a minefield. We were crawling through on our bellies, as usual, locating the mines. Trix had a truly wicked sense of humour at times, and on this occasion he kept poking The Greek and singing to him. The Greek was squirming and telling him to knock it off and getting mad as hell, but the rest of us guys were all just laughing so hard. Finally The Greek just joined in the laughing too. Then we all got back down to the serious business of clearing those mines.

*

One of the guys was a Jewish fella from Brooklyn. He was a tremendous guy and he had that wonderful Jewish sense of humour that just kept on rolling off the tip of his tongue and kept us guys wetting ourselves laughing. Everybody really liked that kid because of the wonderful way that he dealt with life.

When we had left camp back in Fonthill Bishop and decamped to the woods, that little Jewish guy was out on guard duty one night. I remember we pulled up to his post and we weren't challenged. You were supposed to say, 'Halt. Who goes there?' So Sergeant Foster steps forward and says, 'Where are you at?'

He called back, 'I'm behind the tree.'

'What the hell are you doing there?'

He said, 'I don't trust things.'

One of the guys asked him what had happened and he said that he had heard a noise. It was most probably a fox or something, and it scared the crap out of him so he ran behind a tree. We couldn't help but laugh at that and so did he. Needless to say, he wasn't reprimanded because we all liked him so damn much.

Later on, sometime after we landed in Normandy, we were in combat and he got hit in the leg; I was looking over and I saw him clutch his thigh and so he got shipped off home. We used to call it a million-dollar wound. We sure loved that guy and missed his sense of humour.

*

Looking back, it was fierce, intense and dramatic on a daily basis and things very seldom let up. You were in constant battle readiness or involved just about every day; very little of it was quiet and peaceful. Amazingly, a lot of my real close buddies made it home. That sure was a miracle by anyone's standards and we only have the Almighty, who gave us strength and courage, to thank for that.

Chapter 12

Battle of the Bulge

The memory of Christmas 1944 has stayed with me for over seventy years.

With just over a week to the big day the fighting had pretty much come to a halt and so we were just holding the line. We were temporarily based in this big grand house near the centre of Stolberg in what must have been a very posh area at one time. We had set up machine guns, guard posts and roadblocks and things like that. It was bitterly cold and the snow was coming down heavily. We could just about see the Germans way out yonder but they were out of M1 rifle range.

We got pieces of fern and a little Christmas tree, which we decorated the best we could, and we even hung up some army socks and lit the place with candles. We didn't have any presents but what we did have was the spirit of Christmas. We were in the holiday mood and the supply people had dropped off some hot food for us. We were beginning to call a place home for the first time in quite a while. We never truly relaxed because you could never trust what was coming down the pike from the German end, but we were in an easy mood thinking about Christmas, thinking about people back home, family and so on. A lot of the guys started talking about their homes in Wisconsin, North Dakota and other states; they would have their pictures out of their loved ones and take moments off on their own to reflect on their home and family.

It was near midnight and we were in our sacks when Sergeant Foster came around and said, 'Pack up, we're moving out.'

We said, 'What's happening?'

'The Krauts have broken through on our right. Move now.'

That's all he had to say. We packed up and went outside. Now the half-track didn't have a top on it, not like the carriers that you have today, so it was full of snow. We cleaned it out, got in and moved down into the Battle of the Bulge...

Just like the Falaise Gap, the Battle of the Bulge was so called after the war; at the time we just knew it as the Breakthrough. It has also become known as the Ardennes Campaign after the region of Belgium in which it played out. It began on December 16, 1944, when all hell broke loose as the Germans launched a major surprise attack on us Allies, which carried on across Christmas and into the New Year until January 25, 1945. The one thing I didn't need any history book to tell me was that it was one of the worst times we had. Over and above the beaches and the Gap, it was a scary situation to be in and it continued without any let-up. The battle was indescribably ferocious in every respect, with very heavy losses on both sides.

Even though we had supremacy of the air the Germans had timed their attack well. Those sonsofbitches knew that there was no air cover or chance of supplies reaching US forces because the weather was so bad; with heavy snow coming down, we couldn't use our planes because the visibility just wasn't there. The Germans took full advantage of the situation.

There was an infantry division of our boys, which had only just arrived from the United States, and, as a result, were not combat-hardened. The enemy picked them out as a soft underbelly, so to speak. It was very nasty. The Germans really took a lot of those infantry boys' lives because they were so inexperienced. They hadn't been there very long and they were called to hold the line because it was Christmas time. They really tried their best but just didn't have the knowhow, and the line buckled.

The German plan was to quickly get through Belgium and reach a seaport where they could get supplies, especially gasoline.

The battleground was farmland, foothills and thick forest. The weather was bitterly cold—we were absolutely freezing. I had on my trench coat and goodness knows what else while Trix, who was the coldest sonofabitch I had ever seen, must have had three pairs of everything on. Fortunately we had young blood pumping through us and we took what was coming down the pike; we had no alternative, we just moved with it. In truth, we didn't have time to worry about the cold—the killing was nonstop and brutal. I nearly met my maker a number of times in that battle.

I remember travelling through the night, down to the Houffalize area of Belgium, and then, at first light, I got up into my machine gun turret. I saw a lot of infantry boys to our right and, all of a sudden, we were into very heavy small arms fire from the Germans. A lot of fighting was going on all around us so I got busy with my .50 calibre. The Germans were there en masse trying to break through.

Now to all intents and purposes the Battle of the Bulge was a last desperate attempt by the Germans to turn things around and Hitler had ordered that the battle be carried out with a brutality more common on the Eastern Front in order to frighten us; no pity and no prisoners to be taken.

This led to something that really pissed us guys off— the Malmedy Massacre. On December 17, 1944, one SS Panzer division carried out what I see as a terrible crime against humanity.

I didn't witness it first hand, but this is what I heard. The Germans had taken quite a number of our boys prisoner and were transporting them in these big German trucks, which carried around twenty-five to thirty guys each, when they told them that they were stopping for a pee break. All those guys were unloaded into this field and then the Germans dropped down the sides of two of the vehicles to reveal machine guns and they started pouring lead into them. About eighty guys all were murdered apart from, I think, two, who managed to fall into a stream and get away.

Apparently the Germans had been told, 'Take no prisoners. We have got to move forward, we don't have the time or the people to take these prisoners back into Germany and put them into camps.'

The word got back to us about the slaughter. It was not only unacceptable—it was a bloody shock. It was a terrible thing for us guys.

I remember hearing about it and felt the overwhelming desire to even out the score. It precipitated a strong feeling from among us that we would make an extra effort to make things uncomfortable for those bastards.

I have heard that after that, more than a few SS troops or paratroopers failed to be taken prisoner and were shot on sight. As far as my platoon was concerned we were told to use our own judgement. We were very keen to take them out but we did not, to my knowledge, kill prisoners; if we did then we would be the same as them. Saying that, if a prisoner acted like he wanted to spring loose I shot him in the damn legs. I wasn't overly concerned if they had the full blast or not because you get battle-hardened.

It was very difficult to visualise the bigger picture because there was movement going on all around the sector. The intensity of that battle is well known in history, but nothing can adequately communicate the horror, the fear and the killing we witnessed and took part in.

We were moving slowly most of the time. Our recon would say, 'The Krauts are up here.' And we would move up to whatever area we were directed to. One of our first engagements involved three tanks in this big field, it was daylight and there was plenty of snow; it was colder than hell. They were raising all kinds of trouble and we went over there, very gingerly because there was a lot of crap going on all around, and we engaged them. They were SS soldiers; you could always tell the difference because they were much more determined. They were committed to the oath they had taken to the Führer, they were very stubborn and very aggressive; in a sense they were outstanding soldiers, they knew their business, they knew soldiering, they had been at war for years.

We got out of the half-track, because those tanks would have zeroed in on it, and joined the infantry boys. Our half-track driver, Sharp, stayed with the vehicle because it was his responsibility. All our gear was in there, our duffle bags, our gas masks, the explosives, our rations and the water; it was our home, but he got out and crawled under it. It wasn't really safe, but it was safer than being inside.

Myself, Trix, The Greek and some of the other guys decided to take out the tanks that were right near us. I used the bazooka to take out the treads. I always went for the treads because I knew it would do damage. If I went for any other part it could have bounced where it would deflect off it. I would say to Trix, 'Treads!' and the rest of the guys would take out the infantry. We knew automatically what to do. There was no sergeant or officer to direct your every move in the heat of combat.

Trix was behind me with a machine gun and when the Germans came out of the Panzer, he killed them. We moved on to the next tank; one of the infantry used a bazooka on that one, and we waited until the crew inside came out and we killed them. Then we did the same to the third one, which was way out to the right.

After that particular engagement, I went out on a patrol with the infantry trying to get a handle on where the rest of the Germans were. When we found them, we sent the message back to base with our current position, saying we had made contact. When we were returning to base, there was another situation where a tank had been hit but was still using its turret to fire.

Trix got up on that bloody tank and managed to get the hatch open; then he threw in a hand grenade and slammed the sonofabitch down. That took care of that situation.

Getting at a tank was a pretty difficult job, so our guys protected us as we tried. Their own infantry laid down constant fire surrounding these tanks, but you took your chances – that's what being a soldier is all about. You didn't think of the danger, you just thought, 'This sonofabitch is coming at me, I'm going to take it out.' It's automatic and the guys knew exactly what to do. All our guys were firing constantly as there was enemy infantry all around. The whole idea was to get in, kill as many Germans as we could and take over the position that we were after.

Later we set up a roadblock with a couple of half-tracks and a tank standing by, trying to protect our piece of ground and preventing the Germans from getting through.

Word came down, 'Be very careful because they are dressed like us.'

One of the things about the Battle of the Bulge that caused so much confusion was quite a few of these Germans were dressed as Americans and interacting with us. They were very clever, they had our uniforms on and they had American jeeps, and they spoke as if they were Americans; some had even grown up in the States, but they didn't have what the average American has, and that's a good knowledge of American sports, especially baseball.

The guys would say, 'Okay, what unit are you from?'
And they would reel it off.

'Okay,' we would say. 'Let's talk about baseball.'

Of course, we also used to have a daily password and sometimes you could see them hesitating. We didn't run into this sort of thing a lot, but we still had to be constantly at the ready. This one time, a US jeep came down the road and slowed down while the passenger hollered, 'Howdy.'

We stopped the vehicle and there was a driver and three men who turned out to be Germans. It was Sergeant Foster who twigged to it. There was something not quite right about them. When he asked them something and they couldn't answer, he had his gun out straight away and he just started firing. We joined in and we killed all of them.

General George Patton got it damn right when he said, 'Don't you die for your country, let the other sonofabitch die for HIS country.'

*

On Christmas Day 1944 we were out in a very large field, holding our position. We had dug in and there were foxholes all over the damn place. The sun was very bright but there was a lot of snow around. There was some half-hearted small arms fire, but in general, it was quiet. The next thing we knew when we turned around was that there were these supply guys, once again, crawling towards us with big containers of meat and potatoes and stuff. They had brought a turkey dinner, with all the trimmings, out to us from back down the column. It was fantastic, and we were smiling from ear to ear.

When The Greek was handed his, he smiled real big, looked at the guy and said, 'Have you got any more of this crap back there?' He was always hungry.

The fighting had subdued considerably on that particular day, because the Germans respected the Christian aspect of Weihnachten, as they called it. We didn't find that lull in all the killing strange; we half expected it, to be honest, because those guys facing us were also missing their families, their friends and their homes. It was a day of reflection and of not getting too engaged in hostility.

However, the next day we went back to fighting and doing as much damage as we could. When the armoured infantry went out they usually went as a squad of twelve men, plus two engineers. In the Battle of the Bulge the Germans would hide their land mines with a piece of fir tree and the snow would be on top of that, but we could see the bumps in the snow. If we saw anything like that the whole squad would stop and the sergeant would hand signal for the engineers to make their way forward. When the engineers had neutralised the danger, the squad would continue forward.

I swear I nearly got killed on one such patrol. We were in the Schwarzwald, the Black Forest, and it was just full of Germans. It was snowing like hell and way over yonder in a field, we could see something that looked like an airplane that had been shot down. We thought it might be an American bomber, so our mission was to reconnoitre and find out what was going on.

Now, we never talked and we never smoked on patrol; we were dead quiet because our lives depended on it. On this particular occasion, we were walking through the woods and there was a large clearing, right on the edge of the forest, and running alongside was a big expanse of deep pristine snow on which the aeroplane had come to rest.

We were going through those woods and the wind was blowing. How he picked it up I don't know, but just as we were about to leave the cover of those trees and cross the open ground the sergeant, a Tennessee boy who always used to chew tobacco, put his hand up and signalled us to get down. We all dropped and he passed the word back for the engineers to stay in place. There was a machine gun nest with four or five Germans inside, over to our left, in the forest, overlooking the open ground and the aeroplane.

The intenseness of being in that forest, the feeling of combat, of anxiety, knowing that you may not make it back because you are going out there in stealth. It can be overpowering and detrimental if you don't manage it right. But fortunately for little Limey that sergeant was just sharp; he knew how to react. He saved our lives that day. If we had kept on walking and gone into that field we would have been cut to pieces by that machine gun.

The sergeant picked out three guys and they got their hand grenades ready and I saw him count to three silently with his fingers and they all threw at the same time. It killed all those Germans except one. He was bleeding because the shrapnel had caught him, but he would live.

The sergeant said to me, 'Limey, take this fella back to base. They want to interrogate him, we want to know what's going on. Make sure that he stays in line.'

The rest went on to check the aeroplane out while I started walking this German back. It turned out that the aircraft had been there for a while as the bodies inside were decomposing. I don't recall how many of them there were but when I spoke to the sergeant afterwards, he told me there were dead guys in there.

Meantime, I was taking my prisoner back through the woods to our base camp. He was walking in front of me. This guy was a real big bugger. I looked up at him and he just kept going upward—he was at least six and a half foot tall, and I'm about 5'6". We got about half way back to the base and it was snowing something terrible. He stopped and he looked around. He was acting like a real nasty bastard, and then he just sat down—he wasn't going to move. I said, 'Raus.' He just looked at me, spat on the ground and said something in German.

I paused for a minute and thought, 'I'll have you.' I

fired my machine gun right where he was sitting. That sonofabitch got up so fast and jumped so high.

I stopped shooting and said, 'Raus,' again.

He didn't move. He just sat one more time and I just shouted, 'Raus.' By God he looked at me and if he could have killed me he sure would have done me in; he was such a big fella. So I just made him dance a bit with my machine gun. That sonofabitch just kept on dancing because I had the firepower.

He started to move and by then the guys from headquarters had heard my machine gun and sent a squad of infantry to meet us. When that big fella saw all the other guys approaching he behaved. Maybe I should have killed the sonofabitch but I thought, 'No, we need to get some information out of him.'

Now we had Americans who knew how to interrogate. There was no torture and to my knowledge, Americans never tortured their prisoners. First of all they would give them cigarettes or something to eat, they would take good care of them and some of our boys, who were German American, would talk their lingo and let them know that if they gave us the information we would look after them. They'd take them over to Great Britain to a prisoner of war camp where no harm would come to them.

I knew the interrogation officer, and he later told me, 'Limey, it's a good thing you got this fella because there are several platoons of German tanks way over to our left.'

That German blew the whistle on a whole company of soldiers and around fourteen German tanks, quite a concentration of German military that we had no idea about. Our tanks were about three miles down the road, and we were able to notify them in good time and bring them into the action.

I guess what the story illustrates is, because I made a German soldier do the bloody waltz in the snow with my machine gun, that sonofabitch was just dancing and a-moving, we were able to save a lot of our boys' lives.

Throughout it all the weather continued to be absolutely terrible, very cold and snowing, and we still had very little cover from the air force because of the lack of visibility.

One of my closest calls came during that hellhole. We were near this big barn and some Germans were across the yard in the farmhouse. It was late in the afternoon and the exchange of fire had gotten very heavy and a lot of men had been lost on both sides.

We were using up ammunition at quite a rate so Trix, who was using a .30 calibre machine gun, shouted 'Limey. We need more ammo now.'

I nodded, 'Okay, I'll go and get some.'

The half-track was parked outside of the barn. So I went out a side door and was reaching into the half-track for the ammo, which was stored in boxes with handles, and I heard the fizz of a mortar coming in and I hit the deck. I hated mortar fire because it was so unpredictable; you would just hear the wisp and it exploded. All shells explode but with mortar fire there is more shrapnel. It was wicked and there is very little you can do to escape the effects.

It exploded off to my right and a small piece of shrapnel hit my nose and went up into my helmet. It took out one of the little bones or cartilage in my nose and the bleeding was profuse.

I managed to fix it up using my shirt and I grabbed two boxes of ammo and a bandolier of bullets for Trix's .30 calibre, which I slung over my shoulder, and headed back. I just kept wiping the blood away; it wasn't going in my eyes, so I could see all right. The barn door had been blown and Trix looked out and shouted, 'What's happening, Limey?'

'I got hit but I'm all right,' I shouted back.

I crawled back inside the barn and started handing that ammo out and we just carried on. If I hadn't got that ammo we would have been in deep trouble.

In addition to our action there was infantry activity going on to the right and the left of us. There were a lot of GIs all along the line engaged in small arms fire. It was too heavy for me to even think of getting up in the half-track and using my .50 calibre, that would have been suicide.

We were very fortunate that there were no German tanks involved in this particular engagement, just small arms, mortar and artillery fire. Not all engagements were that ferocious, sometimes they just slowed us up, but we were always on alert. If you lost concentration, you could end up dead, or your buddies could.

Another mortar hit the side of the barn and started a fire so we had that to contend with as well; there was too much activity going on to put it out so we just let it burn. We were able to leave our position and move forward before the fire reached us.

After the action had died down a medic asked me what the problem was because I was bleeding. I said a splinter of shrapnel had hit me but I was okay, and that he should take care of the other wounded guys because they were in far worse shape than I was.

I didn't go to the field hospital and no one made a note of it. The field hospital had their hands full. I took a guy back there once; he was in bad shape, and I saw the most horrible sight of our guys who had been hit. They were lying there and some of them were dying, it was terrible. I didn't want to take up the valuable time of the doctors for something that wasn't life threatening.

*

There's one major logistic that tanks, half-tracks, trucks and the like can't do without and that's gasoline. The German gas supplies, or lack of them, were to prove a major turning point during the Battle of the Bulge. So fast was their initial advance that they weren't able to put in place the regular supply lines that forward units need.

Although the Germans had one hell of a lot of tanks and a lot of momentum, it came to an end when they fully realised that they just didn't have enough gasoline to take them to where they wanted to go. So, the key to their continued breakthrough was gasoline, and they were hell-bent on trying to take over our supplies, which we called dumps.

It was a good thing that the American commanders realised this and acted so quickly. Word came down the line that those dumps must not fall into the hands of the enemy.

The cry spread 'Burn the gasoline. Don't let the bastards get it.'

So we blew up our own fuel dumps rather than run the risk of them falling into enemy hands; we had plenty of gasoline back down the line so it wasn't a game changer for us. The dumps were going off like bonfires all around us. That brought them to a standstill. They couldn't move their tanks or vehicles, leaving their infantry wide open.

If the Germans hadn't run out of gas I think that they would have gotten all the way through because they came through in such numbers and with such force; they were thick with Panzers and Tiger tanks. For sure, a lot more GIs would have lost their lives.

The Battle of the Bulge didn't end all of a sudden.

The engagements with the enemy became gradually less intense as we neutralised their forward momentum and began to push them back. Then we finally had the word to move out back into Germany where we regrouped ready to take Cologne.

The surprise attack had caught the Allied forces completely off guard and became the war's costliest battle in terms of casualties for the United States, whose forces bore the brunt of the attack, with around nineteen thousand of the guys losing their lives and more than twice that number being wounded. I wasn't aware of this information at that time—I read about it many years later in our division's official history book, *Spearhead in the West*. I was not at all surprised, though, because I remember the intensity of that battle to this day.

To use the words of *Spearhead in the West*, which says of the battle, 'In the final analysis, it was only because divisions like the 3rd Armored fought to the last cartridge and the last drop of blood and gasoline that Jerry ground to a halt in flame and death and destruction.' The rest is history.

Chapter 13

Central Germany

Shortly after our involvement in the Battle of the Bulge I was riding along in the half-track and I said to Sergeant Foster that I didn't feel at all well; I was lethargic and I was running a nasty temperature.

He said to me, 'Limey, we're going to drop you off in the next village. You can stay there while you recover and the guys following behind will pick you up when you're feeling a bit better.'

The medic who was there had a fair knowledge of medicine although he was not a doctor, and he told me to take aspirin, drink lots of water and to lay low and get plenty of rest.

When we reached the next village, one that had recently been liberated, I was left in a vacant house to recover before re-joining my unit. I think I must have had the flu and I slept for about twenty-four hours. It was still colder than hell and we had been knee-deep in snow for the last few weeks. The guys had left me there and were making their way back to the front near Stolberg. It was a small village and, after all the combat, it was unusually quiet. I felt at times as if I were completely alone in that village.

Not long after waking up I was lying on a settee, when I heard some German voices coming from outside, so I sneaked a peek through the window from behind the curtain. I saw five or six German soldiers making their way down the street. They looked like they were headed right towards the house I was in.

I quickly removed any signs that I was hiding there and went up into the attic and hid myself in a tiny space behind the brick chimney. I got my Colt .45 out in case they came up into the attic to search.

I heard one man poke his head up through the trapdoor and shout, 'Raus. Hande hoch.' (Out. Put your hands up), thinking someone was there.

I thought to myself, 'Do I hit the sonofabitch now?' But I would then have to take on the other four or five guys.

He went back downstairs and sometime later it sounded like they had all left the house. I still lay low for quite a while to be sure. Even after I felt safe again, I stayed up in the attic because it was warm. Eventually, I made my way back downstairs and dozed off to sleep again. I woke sometime the next morning to the sound of Yankee voices. Some guy was yelling, 'Get that damn machine gun over here now.'

I looked out and saw all these American boys and hollered. 'Hey, over here. I need help.'

This big GI came up and said, 'What's wrong with ya?'

I said, 'I've been out of it with the flu for the last couple of days and holed up in this place. My unit left me here and I need to get back to them.'

'What outfit are you with?' he asked.

'The 23rd Armored Engineers,' I told him.

'We're just pulling up the rear here. There's lots more guys coming through. You can stay here for a while longer.'

Pretty soon the house I was in started filling up with GIs and they had K rations with them so I had something to eat. They told me that if I wanted to join them they could get me up to my unit.

I finally got a ride in a jeep, then I got on a half-track and eventually I rode on the back of a tank and finally joined up with my outfit. That was the one time I left my outfit under medical orders to take it easy; I kid you not, I was really, really ill and I didn't want the rest of the guys to catch what I had or for someone to get hurt because I wasn't alert. It all turned out okay and I was able to get back on my feet and, as they say in the army, 'got mean as hell' and re-joined the group.

We were still on the outskirts of Stolberg. We had been in the process of taking it when we had suddenly been ordered down to stop the German breakout now known as the Battle of the Bulge. So, we had to retake some lost ground and secure our position in the city.

After Stolberg, we crossed the River Roer and took a place called Düren without too much trouble, which meant that the prize of Cologne, or Köln to use its German name, was in our sights.

We took it in early March 1945, and in my estimation, that was some of the toughest fighting we saw in the whole war. It was a major German city and they were hanging on for dear life and proving to be a real obstacle to us moving forward.

They had been subjected to plenty of Allied air strikes, because we knew the opposition there would be tremendous, and the devastation was unbelievable. We were accustomed to seeing cities that had been bombed, but this was a whole new level. However, this had not softened up the opposition as hoped.

When we went in with street-to-street fighting it was still dangerous, bloody and vicious. One of the problems we had in taking it was that the primary bridge into the city had been destroyed. It was a big bridge; it had to be replaced by a pontoon bridge to allow access for our tanks and other vehicles. This was a hell of a difficult task with heavy fighting everywhere. Although my squad weren't directly involved with constructing the pontoon bridge, we were in the thick of the fighting with the infantry that enabled the other engineers to complete the task.

I was shown some film footage of the 3rd Armored Division moving into the city. You can clearly see the devastation, the streets are piled high with the rubble from burnt-out buildings yet, miraculously, there in the middle if it all are the majestic spires of Cologne Cathedral which managed to survive the bombing. It brought back a hell of a lot of memories. There is also some famous footage of a German Panzer tank being taken out and you can see those inside frantically trying to escape the flames and being shot.

I couldn't watch it all the way through. At one point you see some GIs covering up a dead German woman. Some things you just need to forget; but I never will.

*

Just as we were really getting stuck into the treasured Rhineland of Germany, right at the end of March 1945, Spearhead was dealt a crushing blow with the loss of our much-respected general, Maurice Rose. From what I heard he was way up front, as always, when his jeep ran into a German tank. With a cannon pointing down on him and his driver, he had no choice but to surrender. Apparently he reached down for his sidearm to hand it over to the tank commander, who misunderstood, because that German shot him.

We weren't very far away when the news came through. We were deep into Germany and General Rose, being the man he was, was never very far away from his men. He was a unique officer, a soldier's soldier. He literally worked his way up from a buck private to a two-star general. He was always, without exception, interested in the guys who were holding the line, more so with the ordinary soldier than with the officers. He really cared about how we were doing in terms of food and ammunition, how we were feeling, where we were from. He had a heart brimful of compassion. When he would pass by in his jeep he would ask, 'Okay guys? Everything all right?' Sometimes he would stop and come over and take a look at the situation. 'How's things going here?' He would evaluate the situation and go back to his jeep and get hold of his staff and explain what he had just seen.

I saw him once right in the middle of a damned tank battle. There must have been twenty or thirty tanks on either side and they were really blasting away and he was standing up in his jeep. He was communicating to the tank commander with his hands and using the jeep's field radio to direct the battle. Most of us were hunkered down in our half-tracks, and could hear the barrage of ammunition, which was exploding all over the damn place. I was up in the gun turret, directing our driver and firing my .50 calibre, so I had a good view of the general in action.

He was a first-class decent human being and respected by his troops. He didn't shout like Patton and some other generals did. He was just a relaxed ordinary guy, the kind of guy that you would give your life for. When he died, and the way in which he died, it was a shock to all of us.

Many years later, I was asked to speak at one of the 3rd Armoured Division's reunions in Fort Knox, Kentucky. I felt compelled to speak again about what a wonderful person he was, and what a great leader. He really was one of us.

*

After Cologne we went up to a place called Paderborn. Once the Germans had been pushed back we were able to slow up to catch our breath, as it were. Paderborn was home to the central storage unit of the German Army. It was a supply depot that used a system of tunnels as storage space. We saw underground rooms full of uniforms, both male and female; beyond that there were ammunition, tobacco, wine, even chocolate, it went on and on. It was a supply depot in every sense of the word.

It was also home to an airfield with Stuka bombers and all kinds of German aircraft. When we took Paderborn it was one of those lightning strikes and some of those planes had been abandoned with the engines still running. Our intelligence had told us that the place would be heavily fortified because of the supplies there but they were wrong; those pilots skedaddled, our aircraft were up there already and they probably thought it safer to run on foot.

After the intensity of the battle had quietened down, we were finally able to relax a little. We were near a couple of those planes with their engines running so I climbed up into one cockpit and Trix got up into the other one. It was one of those deals where having never been inside a fighter plane I was curious as to what it was like. It had these dials and all kinds of levers, knobs, buttons and pedals. As I pulled back on one lever the bloody thing started revving. I looked out and saw the lieutenant and he was hollering something at me, slitting his throat with his hand telling me to kill the engine. I didn't pay any attention to him; I just wanted a go at it. It started to move and I pulled this knob out a little further and it began to move faster. I looked across to my right and saw that Trix was already moving. He saw me looking and he saluted me.

I found that by playing with the brakes you could go different ways and you could play around with the wheel. I didn't know what the hell I was doing and I hit a button and the bloody machine gun went off. Thank God the bullets went up into the sky and didn't hurt anyone. It was just one burst but it scared the hell out of me. So I stopped the engine and got out. Trix was already out; he had hit something with his aeroplane. Lieutenant Norwood came running over and said in his deep southern accent, 'What the hell do you guys think you were doing? I can have you court-martialed.'

'What for?' I asked. 'All we did was get into these aeroplanes to see what they were all about.'

'Get back to your squad,' he said.

And we took off with our tails between our legs to where the rest of the guys were watching and they cheered us no end; they had been down the tunnels and gotten hold of the champagne so we all had a toast to our victory.

I should mention here that I had picked up a camera from a dead German officer near Omaha Beach; it was up near the top somewhere around Isigny. We had engaged some Germans and quite a few had got killed and the rest of them surrendered. I walked over and had a look at these guys and I saw the camera.

It was a Leica. It had a good lens on it and some film. I thought to myself, 'I'll hold on to this.'

After that, I kept my eye out for a shop to get some film, which I did eventually. Getting the films developed was another matter. If I left the film in a shop overnight we might have to leave before I could pick it up, so I kept these rolls of film and when we were stabilised, that's when I took some to be developed. The German behind the counter did it for free. I carried that camera with me throughout the war and took it back to the States with me. I eventually gave it to one of my children. Anyway, one of the guys took a photograph on my liberated camera of me sat in that cockpit that I still have today.

When we got into those tunnels we loaded up with chocolate and cigars, much of which had been taken by the Germans from Paris and places like that and stashed down there. There was tons of the stuff. I didn't see any oil paintings or things like that but they went into banks and took money, they went into art galleries and took works of art, that's just the way it was.

While we were exploring those tunnels we were in one room when Trix called out, 'Hey, Limey, look at this.'

I turned around and he had a pair of ladies' bloomers on.

'What do you think of these?' he asked. They came down to the knees.

'They look good,' I said.

'They sure are warm,' he said, 'you want a pair?'

'Sure.' He threw me a pair and I put them on.

The Greek saw me and said, 'Where the hell did you get those?'

I said, 'Trix has them over there.' And he went and got himself a pair too. Then the horsing around started. We were dancing around, and the other guys were clapping and laughing. It was a rare opportunity to blow off some steam after all the intensity of battle. I still smile when I think about that time, but it didn't last long. Soon we were back in the thick of it.

It was so bloody cold that we kept those bloomers, and wore them under our pants to help keep that bone-piercing cold out; luckily we didn't catch a bullet and have to be taken to the field hospital, only for the medics to get the wrong idea.

After Paderborn we assisted in mopping up the Ruhr Valley, crossed the River Saale, and, after overcoming stiff resistance yet again, we took a town called Dessau. We were on a roll, as they say, but the wind was soon to be blown the hell out of our sails and it had nothing to do with those 88s or German tanks.

If ever we needed any reminder that we were indeed engaged in a fight between good and evil then it came in the form of the horror that we saw in early April 1945, when we had taken the German town of Nordhausen. Although not a major town, in the few days before approaching the area the resistance was intense; we were facing the SS elite rather than the old men and kids that had been drafted into so many previous situations. The reason became clear when we came out on top and discovered they had been protecting a death camp.

The Spearhead infantry had taken the camp, with the engineers bringing up the rear, to discover a concentration camp. Although I was not there when it was first taken, I still saw too much and it had such an impact on my life. Nordhausen was a hellhole in every sense of the word. The Nazis had developed an efficient killing machine, and it was sickening and overwhelming to us, even after the many horrors we had already seen and experienced throughout the war. The term 'death camp' was a good description.

I can never forget the look in the eyes of those people and how they were dressed in rags, when it was so cold.

It kind of explained the heavy resistance of those bastards. They must have known that when we had control of that camp, and saw what had been going on, that we were going to start taking prisoners and that we weren't going to be very kind to them.

There wasn't a wall. It was just huts on a big field with barbed wire all around it. I went up to the gate and looked inside. I had no inclination to go inside that camp; it wasn't a sightseeing tour. I saw enough from the entrance of it. I don't think my guts would have taken it, to be honest. It was terrible, the amount of people who were inside that camp, and they were dying before our eyes. There were many bodies littered on the ground. More lay in the barracks in contorted half-naked heaps. The stench of rotting human flesh was horrendous and never goes away.

A few of the prisoners were coming up to us. They were skin and bones, walking skeletons; I put my arm around one of them and it was like touching bones. Some were dropping like flies, yet they had smiles on their faces because they had been liberated. As they were dying they knew that they had been freed.

They were dying from lack of water, lack of food, from the lack of a lot of things. While the camp had been under siege for three or four days, there had been no water or anything for them, but they had clearly not been fed proper food for a very long time. One poor soul came up to me gesturing for me to give him something to eat. I started giving him some of my rations and Sergeant Foster said, 'You better hold up on that until the medics see them.' Apparently too much food would hurt them as their bodies had been starved and could not process the solid food at that point. Our medics and doctors went in there but there wasn't a lot they could do for most of them, they were that far gone.

You couldn't talk to these guys because of the language difficulty and they were dying. Some of these poor guys tried to get at the few Germans guards who were left but we had to stop that, although they had every right to be pissed off with their captors.

I believe most of them were either Russians or Polish. It was hard to tell whether they were Jewish or not to be honest, but we know from history that many of them were of the Jewish faith.

Later I was standing by the half-track with the rest of the guys, when one of the liberated men came up to me. He was a tall guy yet so skinny you could see his bones. He shook my hand and said, 'Danke schön, mein herr.' Then he quietly sat down and he died right there.

The reaction to what we saw got to me at rather a deep level—to see how human beings could treat other human beings. I was a young man doing what I was paid to do. It was a job and that's the way I looked at it but when I came upon all this, it was such a terrible experience that I never got over it—those sights have stayed with me all of my life.

Our generals went in there. I think sometime later Eisenhower went in to see for himself. Certainly some very important military people went in to take a look at this and to make their assessment on what was going to be done after the war. I heard that later, after we had moved on, they made the German civilians go in there and take a look at what their beloved Fuhrer had done.

*

Each battle that I was in personally, everything that we had seen and done, had served to make us harder. Those sights, and the things we had to do, they change a man on the inside. It had this impact on us, but it only made us more determined to bring this war to an end. It was a ferocious battleground as we drove deeper into Germany. It was their home country and we were the first to invade it. It didn't go down well with them and they knew it was their last stand. It felt like each battle from that point on grew more and more intense.

*

Although we were within striking distance of Berlin by the end of April 1945, we did not go into the German capital. We skirted around it and went up towards the River Elbe, where we were supposed to meet the Russians. It was around about this time that I heard that

Hitler had committed suicide. I remember thinking, 'Good riddance to a bunch of crap' because that was all he was.

*

When we reached the Elbe, orders came down from headquarters to stop right there and not to cross. We didn't. We were back to holding the line and within a few hours the Russians turned up and it was they who came across the river. They had finally met up with elements of the Allied forces moving through Germany and seemed elated that the Americans were on the other side of the river; when they came across they brought their happiness with them.

The number of women in their ranks surprised me; it seemed to me that they had been driving the tanks. They were big women—they weren't fat, they were just big ladies. They were pretty looking but like all of us in combat uniform, they hadn't had a good bath in months.

Now the Russian people express their happiness by hugging you so you can imagine little Limey being picked up by these giants in a bear hug. I started shaking hands with one of the women and she just picked me up into a hug.

There was a lot of slapping on backs and shaking of hands and dancing. I heard them singing and they were doing that Russian dance on bended knees. It was a few hours of happiness, on both sides, that we had met up. Some of our generals were also there and I remember thinking, 'Something significant is happening here.'

I didn't know where the hell the Russians had come from but there we were meeting them and enjoying the moment with them. I thought, 'Here's the Allies, where do we go from here? Perhaps this might be the end of things in Europe.' As it turned out, within a couple of days the war in Europe had finished.

It was a few days after, as we were making our way back, that we officially heard that the war was over. We were in the half-track. There wasn't a lot of celebrating going on, just relief.

I don't remember any parties at the time. Later there were victory parades in places like London and Paris, but we didn't get any of that, all the flowers and the hugging, at all. We were certainly pleased that the war was over and there was a relief that combat was over, although there was still some spasmodic fighting going on because they hadn't got the word, but we didn't give it much thought; most of the guys were thinking, 'I gotta get home. I want to see my family and wife.' Not the fact, 'Hey, we won a war.' We just wanted to get back to America and get on with life.

Then we heard that we were going to get ready to go to the Pacific where the war was still very much ongoing. We were going to go back to the United States to be re-outfitted and moved to California and then over to the

Japanese combat situation. I didn't feel comfortable with that because we had been through hell for the best part of a year.

My Division had lost over two and a half thousand men, with around three times that number ending up wounded, over a total of two hundred and thirty-one days of combat, so, to be honest with you, our attitude was, 'Oh crap, here we go again.'

Chapter 14

Army of Occupation

As it turned out the United States Air Force paid a visit to Hiroshima and Nagasaki and that pretty much put a stop to any talk of us going across to the Pacific and brought an end to the war in general. I remember one of the guys telling us about it. I didn't know what the hell an atomic bomb was, I just knew that it was some kind of super bomb. I was just glad that it was all over.

Having said goodbye to our new Russian buddies we had left the River Elbe and headed for the town of Darmstadt, which is around thirty miles south of Frankfurt, to start preparations for the Pacific. Thankfully, with the surrender of the Japanese, the role for some of us was changed to being part of the Army of Occupation. Things couldn't just return to normal after the most destructive war ever seen. There were consequences and there was work to be done to rebuild.

We were housed in a large school, which had survived the bombing by some miracle. For us guys, that meant saying goodbye to that old gal, the half-track. For just shy of a year from the beaches of Normandy to the heart of Germany, she had been our home as well as a fighting machine and I will never forget the times I spent up there in the turret on the .50 calibre with my life on the line. Now, new troops were coming over from the United States to help with the reconstruction of Europe, and all of our equipment was handed over to them to aid their mission.

There was evidence of combat everywhere. The towns, villages, and especially the big cities, had really taken a hammering. The civilians lived wherever they could. Many would go back and find that their homes had been destroyed so they would try and get into the basement and clean it out the best they could and make it liveable; that's just the way it was. It was so sad, and now that the war was over, we felt genuinely sorry for them, and gave them as much assistance as we could.

One of our biggest responsibilities was to help the hundreds of thousands of people who were on the move, going back to their homes in France, Belgium, Poland and so on. Most of them were on the streets, day and night. For the most part, they were without food, water or other basic necessities of daily life. Part of our job was to help the police to manage this large movement of displaced people. There was little or no public transportation, and normal facilities like grocery stores and places to eat were, for the most part, just not open or available. Even if they had been, the people had little or no money. We had to help to set up distribution networks for food and basic supplies so these people could survive. Like most of the GIs, seeing the children with no food, nothing, particularly moved me. We just couldn't stand to see them suffering.

Families and friends had been uprooted and separated by the conflict. There were central points in Darmstadt and other towns and cities throughout Europe with information boards with names of people trying to contact each other. Local authorities ran these with significant Allied assistance. Our function was to help re-establish order. This was primarily the responsibility of the military police, and we worked with them in many ways. This included helping civilians to relocate back to their homes peacefully. We also helped out when the inevitable fights broke out over scarce supplies.

One of the things we were particularly on the alert for were the SS soldiers who were putting on civilian clothes and trying to blend in to escape us. We could often spot them because they were healthy young men who stood out from the rest of the civilian population. Sometimes we got considerable help from the locals, who often hated the SS as much as we did. There was an attitude that stayed with the SS; they had lost the war and were trying to save their skins and that made them very dangerous.

Initially the German people were too scared to come out of their homes and onto the streets. Many of them thought that they were going to be shot, raped or God knows what. Another reason for their reluctance was you had some of those prisoners from the labour camps running around all over the place in their prison garb and they wanted revenge. They wanted to beat up the Germans, and any Germans would do. They took out their anger on German civilians. If they found a German walking around, they would beat the living hell out of him. Of course, we had to try to put a stop to things like that, which they didn't like, but despite being angry, when they were looking at a M1 rifle they usually knew when to back off.

*

A big part of the Army of Occupation's role was to build up a democratic system of local government for the Germans and to maintain law and order, which proved to be a very large undertaking. We set up a political system where we would get hold of the lord mayor and his cronies who used to run the town or the village and helped them rebuild. We had officers who spoke German and were experienced in military rule.

*

The weeks that followed were reconciling the fact that the war had finished. These were civilians here, most of them were starving, most of them needed medical and dental attention, the education system was all out of whack, etc. They had absolutely nothing, which, bearing in mind my childhood back in Swansea, I could relate to.

I remember there was a factory in Darmstadt that used to make canned peaches or pears. The civilians were really scrambling to get in there because there were shed loads of cans. We were supposed to stop them but we turned a blind eye to that so they could get something to eat. We were pretty mindful that people needed that kind of help.

*

The German civilians we encountered were, on the whole, nice people. Trix and The Greek and me used to go over to this little village where we got friendly with the people. We used to give them our 10 in 1 rations to help them out. The kids were given more chewing gum and candy than you could shake a stick at.

There was also a PX on our base where we could go and buy candy, chocolate Hershey bars, cigarettes and some types of food. At times we used to buy this stuff and give it to the villagers.

One day Trix said to me, 'Hey, Limey, I know how we can get into the PX.'

'How are you going to do that?' I asked.

'We're moving in tonight,' he said.

When it was dark we went around the back and there was a storeroom window left slightly open. Now we were agile in those days and we were through that damn window before you could say Jack Robinson; there was all kinds of stuff inside.

I said to Trix, 'If we take it easy, and not take too much stuff out of here, we will be okay for weeks.'

We just took a little of this and a little of that and gave it away to the German people. It was in Darmstadt, after the war, that Trix got his stripes. He was made corporal, as I recall. There's a photograph of Trix and me with him pointing to his stripes with a big grin on his face. Do you know what the first thing was that he said to me after getting those stripes?

'Hey, Limey,' he said, 'go and make me a cup of coffee.'

I told him to bugger off.

*

Life sure was mighty fine compared to the hell we had been through. There was some military to it; you couldn't lie in bed until all hours of the morning, you still had to get up at 6:30 a.m., clean the place and get ready for whatever instructions were coming down, but compared to before, it was heaven. It was peaceful, it was the end of the war, and the guys were making plans to go back home to their sweethearts, their moms and dads, brothers and sisters.

We were allowed to have a transatlantic telephone conversation with our families, and as I didn't have any family in the United States I used mine to call Dr Race in Staten Island. I had tried to keep in touch the best I could and wrote to him occasionally through the Army Post Office system. At Paderborn I had taken a big box of cigars, from those underground stores, and managed to wrap them up and sent them back to Dr Race.

*

Going into June the weather was good. Darmstadt was a very big town and next to it was a little village with a big pool where the Germans used to go down to swim and sunbathe. I used to go down as well and I met quite a few German people, especially the fräuleins; there were very few German guys, just some sixteen- or seventeen-year-old younger guys. Most of the German men were either in prison camps or were dead.

Although the Germans were a little reluctant to socialise with us, among us Americans there was little or no hostility left by this point. Instead there was a general feeling of 'we're through, we're finished, we're going home soon'. However, the US Army had some rules about what they called fraternising with the German civilians. We all tried to follow this, but it was a difficult policy to adhere to at times.

I had a girlfriend over there in that village. I was kind

of sweet on her, by golly, but the only way I could see her was after dark. If her own people caught her fraternising she would be in a whole heap of trouble too. By this time, I knew my way to her village even in the dark; I could have gone over there blindfolded. Trix and The Greek had girlfriends over there as well so the three of us would get together and make arrangements to meet up and walk back together. We never got hurt or attacked because we kept it quiet.

We had met at that pool where we used to go swimming. We were young GIs and we hadn't been in the company of women for months and months. It was a pleasure getting to know these girls. They would invite you back to their homes for a black drink that tasted like coffee but it was made from some beans that they had roasted in a frying pan over the fire. They called it Mooga Vouch and it tasted lousy but we used to drink it anyway. Their families were polite and sociable, but they didn't want their neighbours knowing that we were visiting.

*

I met this one girl who spoke some English. She was engaged to a German tank officer; she was still very much in love with him, as I could understand, but we became very good friends. I don't know where he was but he wasn't there. She invited me home and introduced me to her family. Her father looked very ill.

I said to the old man, 'Problem?'

'Yes,' he said, 'heart.'

I thought to myself, 'How the hell can I help this fella?'

The civilians had very few doctors; they had all been called into the service. It was very difficult to get hold of any medicines. The pharmacies weren't open, everything had been disrupted because they had taken one hell of a pounding, so I took him to the field hospital and asked a doctor for help.

He said there wasn't much he could do. I said, 'Just try.'

He said. 'Who the hell are you?'

I said, '23rd Armored Engineers, 3rd Armored Division.'

He replied, 'Oh, you guys have really been through it. Out of respect for that, I'll do what I can.'

He checked the old guy out with his stethoscope and told me that he was in bad shape and needed some drug or other for his heart.

He said, 'He's going to need digitalis.'

I said, 'Where is he going to get that?'

He looked at me and said, 'You see that cupboard? There's some in there,' and he gave him enough to see him through for a while.

*

Towards the end of July word came through to get ready to go to these camps in the south of France. They were all named after American cigarette brands; you had Camp Chesterfield, Camp Lucky Strike and Camp Camel. They were very large and held the contingencies of American troops waiting to get on those ships to go back home. I was bloody elated; I thought, 'I'm going back to the States!' But then the captain came up to me and said, 'Limey, you ain't going any place.'

I said, 'I don't understand.'

He then explained the points system, which I didn't know anything about. To my understanding, they allocated one point per month you were in the service and I think there were additional points if you were married or had children. When you had accumulated enough you would be sent home. I asked when my buddies would be moving out and he said in a couple of days.

Now Trix and The Greek had been in the army at least six months ahead of me. They had joined the 3rd right from the start up in Louisiana and had trained in California's Mojave Desert and the hills of Virginia. I hadn't gotten involved until a few months later, up in Camp Indiantown Gap, so I didn't have enough points. When I told the guys the news they didn't like it one bit but you can't fight the system.

The three of us got together and had a few drinks and had some good talks about the times we had spent together, both in the States and the war in Europe. We reminisced a lot and made a commitment that when we were all back in the States, and things had settled down with our lives, we would make an effort to contact each other and stay in touch.

I said to The Greek, 'I know how to get Trix in Pennsylvania, but how are we going to get hold of you?'

He said, 'Don't worry, Limey; I'll be in touch, no problem.'

The last thing Trix said to me before leaving was, 'Hey, Limey, where's that hundred dollars you owe me?'

I said, 'I'll tell you what, Trix, do you trust me?'

'Yeah,' he said.

'Then I will put it in the mail.'

And we shook on it.

*

Although the war was over, there were still plenty of mines and other explosives left around the countryside, and these needed to be made safe. Civilians would report these to us from time to time.

One time, some villagers came to us and said there were mines over yonder in one of the nearby fields. We followed them and, sure enough, there was a small minefield there. We got to work defusing the mines and after a while I removed this tiny detonator out of one of the teller mines, and it didn't look quite right to me. I took it over to the sergeant and said, 'There's something not right with this detonator.'

Now these detonators were a little over an inch long and thin as a pencil, and they had to be removed from the mines very carefully. There was a pin that held the firing mechanism back, and when disturbed it would fire a small charge to set off the main explosive, which was the mine itself. Removing this holding pin was how you deactivated the detonator. Normal procedure was to take the pin out with it pointing away and discharge it. I held it out in my hand, and as the pin looked different than I had seen before, I was looking directly at it. While I was examining the pin, it moved and the detonator went off, shooting its explosive force directly into my face.

Just before it happened one of my new buddies was taking pictures on my camera, and I have still got one of me holding the detonator, in my hand, just before it went off.

As soon as it happened, the sergeant grabbed me and laid me down and called the medic.

He said, 'What's wrong, Limey?'

I said, 'I can't see nothing.'

I ended up in a hospital in Nice, in the southern part of France, but can't remember getting there. I was in the hospital for six or seven weeks. I believe they used a strong magnet to pull the splinters out. I was blind for some time and I was scared senseless that I would never see again. I thought that that was the end of things. Then the doctor told me that he had good and bad news. He said that I would be able to see again but not as well as before; my sight would come back gradually.

All of the staff were wonderful, and very reassuring. The nurses took good care of me and worked hard to keep my spirits up, although I couldn't see them.

Initially they had both my eyes bandaged. After a few weeks they took one bandage off. Then several weeks later the other came off. The sight in one eye has always been a bit blurred by it but thankfully I have been okay. I take things as they come and whatever's being dished out is dished out. It had always been my attitude towards life, and I think this just reinforced it. I believe that a positive attitude is the best way to live and it has seen me through some very tough times.

*

By the time I got back to Darmstadt, Trix and The Greek and the rest of my old outfit had long since arrived home and I was now assigned to the 93rd Field Artillery. The next morning the captain wanted to see me. He said, 'Limey, you have done one hell of a good job. I appreciate everything that you have done, so anything that you want, you've got it.'

I said, 'What do you mean?'

He looked at me and said, 'Any job you want, because you guys have been through hell. You say what you want. Just name it. We're going to sort it out now.'

I had a little think and I said, 'Well, I'd like to drive a jeep.'

The new captain said, 'Can you drive?'

I said, 'Yeah.' I was lying like hell but I thought with a jeep I could travel around and see places.

'Limey, you've got it.'

They gave me the job. I went to the motor pool and took one of the jeeps out. I wasn't a complete stranger to it and thought to myself, 'Yeah, I can do this.'

A couple of days later I had to take the new lieutenant down to some other town. We got on the highway and he kept looking at me and he eventually said, 'Hey, Limey, you're still in first gear.'

'Oh,' I said, 'alright, I'll change that.' And I put it into second.

He looked at me and said, 'You haven't been driving much have you?'

I said, 'I haven't been driving at all.'

'But you said you could drive?'

'Yeah, but I was lying.'

He laughed and said, 'Just take it easy.'

He helped me along and by the time we arrived I was driving pretty well.

When we stopped he said, 'I've got to go to this very important meeting. Pick me up at 1600 hours.'

It was his turn to tell a lie—he had a girlfriend down there.

*

Being a driver in the Army of Occupation turned out, for me, to be a strange time. I didn't really know what to expect. Finally, I didn't have the constant pressure of being on the line with tanks and infantry and combat engineers, that kind of thing, so I was able to relax somewhat, if you will. It was rest and recuperation and a kind of pat on the back from the upper echelons for the guys who had already been through so much and done a great job. I didn't have to get up at the crack of dawn. There was little regimentation. I could get up at a reasonable time. When the other guys were getting up and moving, I would get up to shoot the breeze, and we would get some breakfast. The day before, the lieutenant would let me know what was coming the next day.

They were very keen that I wore my class A uniform as the officers always looked very, very sharp, and expected the same of me. However, once I had dropped off the officers, my time was my own. I had the freedom to go to different places until I needed to be back to pick them up. I was very dependable, never late or anything, but I was also able to relax, which was a wonderful thing after all I had been through.

I remember one time, I was driving down the highway in my jeep, and there was a family including a young girl drudging down the road carrying all of their worldly possessions. It was a sad sight, and I stopped to see if I could help. With my very limited German and some hand signs, I managed to understand that they were headed to a village outside the town. Although we were not supposed to do so, I loaded them into the jeep and drove them the fifteen or so miles to the village. When we arrived, they were kissing my hands in gratitude, which was embarrassing really—I had only done what was right and human. I saw a lot of the GIs there doing the same thing. It just came naturally.

*

After Trix and The Greek left I was working with a whole bunch of guys who were fresh from the United States and I would try and make them understand about getting along with the locals and how they must feel about us being there in their country. We needed to work with them, and if we were going to be accepted by the Germans then we would have to be friendly. I said to myself, 'Cliff, you're a friendly guy anyway,' and that's what I did.

I thought to myself, what the hell can I do to make these people realise that the Allied troops are not monsters, we are not there to torture, we are not there to maim; we are there to help try and make their lives a bit better. Then an idea struck me.

I got talking to an old man in this little village, across a field from us, and he asked me, 'Have you any food?'

I asked, 'What's going on?'

He said, 'The whole village has very little food. Is there any way that you can help us?'

'I don't have any food right now, but I'll see what I can do,' I told him. I asked him to show me where he lived, and he did.

After I left him, I got to thinking about how I could help him and the rest of the villagers. It occurred to me that there were a lot of deer in the Black Forest, and this might help solve the problem. So I went up there very early the next morning, when the deer came out to feed, and shot two or three with my rifle and put them on my jeep. The Germans were forbidden to have guns and nobody was allowed to hunt in that forest during the war. Someone told me that it had been Hermann Goering's forest and you mustn't shoot there, but that didn't bother me none.

I took them to this old man and we cut them up and gave meat to the village. From then on, I used to do that occasionally in the mornings, as time allowed. Then I asked the old man if he liked fish.

'Yes,' he said.

Not too far from us was a major river. So I went down

there with my jeep and I saw this fella working on his boat and, with my limited German, I asked him if he would take me out to fish. He said yes but then looked at me and said, 'Where's your rod?'

'I don't need that, just take me out,' I replied.

We got halfway across and I told him to stop. I had a couple of hand grenades and I pulled the pins and threw them way out into in the river. There were several explosions, sending water up in the air but once it settled there were fish coming up all over the place.

If you could have seen the look on that guy's face when I popped those hand grenades—he thought he was gonna die. After all the fish came up, he was laughing so hard I thought he would wet himself. This fella had a net and we hauled them all on board.

Back on land I had a big tarpaulin in the back of the jeep and we dumped them in. I told him to take some but he said he can get them with his reel and asked if I had any gasoline. I said yes and gave him a jerry can of gas. After that he took me out whenever I wanted as long as I had some gas to spare.

I took all that fish back to that old man in the village. His wife was very ill, and they had a son who was in the army and a daughter living at home who was about my age. I gave them all the fish to share with the rest of the village. As with the deer, I would do this occasionally. I'd go down to the river to see the guy with the boat, who turned out to be an okay kind of guy, and get some fish.

Nobody knew what I was doing but I couldn't care less if it got me in trouble. It was after the war and there were very few demands upon that jeep and me. It was just one of those things of doing what you could to help people. That's just how it was; I guess you could say I went from killing to helping people. It was just the right thing to do in my book.

*

In all I spent six months in the Army of Occupation before word came down, in late November 1945, that I had finally collected enough points to go down to Camp Chesterfield in southern France and from there, back to the United States. Once I got there I was taken ill and ended up in the hospital again for a week or so. I missed one ship, but was eventually able to get aboard and head for home.

When the ship arrived in the States, heading into New York harbour, the tug came out to meet us, and sounded the horn. It was taken up by the other ships to welcome home the troops. Even though it was six months after the end of the war, they still gave us a great heroes' welcome. People would line the docks to meet their loved ones and welcome the soldiers home. When I saw the Statue of Liberty, I swelled with pride. It really brought home to me that I was about to start my new life in my new country.

Chapter 15

The United States of America

After arriving back in the United States I spent a week or so in Fort Dix, New Jersey, being processed out of the Army and, to be honest with you, I couldn't wait to get out. There was this guy on a typewriter asking me about my service, where I had been trained, where I had been stationed and the campaigns I had served in so he could make notes for my army record. Once he had finished he paused and said, 'I have something for you.'

'What's that?' I asked.

'Well, here it is,' he said, handing me an envelope.

I opened it slowly and a big smile came over my face and I said to myself, 'By golly. I'm now officially American.' It was my certificate of US citizenship, which I had been promised back when I first joined the army. I hung on to that for dear life. I was then handed my discharge papers along with, as I recall, something like $100 to tide me over. Then I found myself on the street carrying what few possessions I had in my duffle bag. I had my whole future ahead of me at that point and I was determined to make something of myself.

I was still in uniform and wore it for a couple of weeks until I had enough spare money to go to the JCPenney department store in New York and get myself a pair of britches and some shirts. Walking around in that uniform the Americans would come up to you and shake your hand, put their arm around you and say things like, 'Thanks for doing a good job. You're a hero.' If you were in a bar they would say, 'Don't touch your money; let me get that for you.' It gave me the feeling that at least I had done something of value here in fighting for the United States.

Needing somewhere to live, I headed back to Staten Island to stay with Dr Race. He still treated me like family and we had quite a time catching up; he wanted to hear all about my adventures during the war. I asked him if he had gotten the cigars that I had sent him from Paderborn. He had indeed and said, 'Those were very good cigars but I was too scared to smoke them in case they exploded because they are German.'

I asked, 'Do you still have them?'

'Yes,' he said. They had a damp towel wrapped around them and they were in the icebox.

I said, 'Pull them out and let's smoke one.'

'You smoke first,' he said.

I did, and they tasted great.

Dr Race really was a wonderful human being; he gave me some insight into what I should be looking at in terms of a career and getting on with life. What I really needed was a job right away; I didn't want to be a burden on Dr Race or anybody else for that matter. Eventually I decided to go into the American Merchant Service, as a fireman, on coastal oil tankers going from Manhattan down to Texas and places like that. I wasn't there for long, only around nine months or so, but I really enjoyed being back at sea.

I also had some personal problems to overcome as I set about building myself a new life. What I didn't realise, at first anyhow, was that right then, because of the war, I was in bad shape mentally. The aftermath of combat takes its toll on any sane-thinking human being and I had been in combat for a very long time. I would often think of the number of young German mothers getting the news that their sons had been killed; just like the British and American mothers. I was responsible for the deaths of a lot of young German soldiers and was fully aware of the pain that had caused their families. That weighed heavy on me, the tremendous agony that is caused by war.

It's difficult to convey to another human being the feelings and emotions that arise, not necessarily at the time of combat, but certainly afterwards. The thing is, very few people understand the extreme responsibility of taking a life. In a wartime situation this is what it's all about but it doesn't stop when the war stops. Unless an individual has experienced combat and the finality of having to take the life of another person, they cannot understand. It doesn't stay back there where it happened;

it comes back to haunt you in unexpected ways for the rest of your life.

I had dreams going back to the campaigns, the slaughter and bloodshed, the hedgerow fighting; it all became a reality again in my mind. I needed medical help. There had been a holdover in my mind of all the nasty things I had seen. It doesn't leave you; it stays there and is very difficult to come to terms with.

Truth be told, although in my ninety-sixth year, I have never really managed to come to terms with the horrors I witnessed during my time in combat and still have nightmares to this day.

One of the most vivid ones is the time we took this large block of apartments, killing a lot of German soldiers getting to the top of that building. For some reason, I have to go back out to the half-track to get something or other. I make my way down the stairs and as I pass one landing a door opens and this massive German comes at me. We are talking one of the biggest people I had ever seen in my life; he is like a damn bear, who, if he gets his hands on me, there's no doubt in my mind that he will tear me apart in seconds.

I react immediately. I have my Colt .45 in my hand and I am able to draw it up just as he is about to grab hold of my throat. I shoot the guy in the chest and it blows a large hole in him; if a .45 hits you, then you stay hit. If I had been a split second slower there's no way I would be here now.

The dream really scares me and the worst thing about it all is that it actually happened.

I'm not a drinking man, and never have been, but I drank rather heavily when I left the army to try and drown it all out. I drank and drank for about nine months or so. I turned to drink and I couldn't get myself together. At times I would get through a small bottle of scotch a day, which for little ole me was unheard of.

Things came to a head when I went to a bar on Staten Island one night with a group of friends. They later found me outside passed out on a bench by a bus stop. I had messed myself and didn't know where the hell I was. I was just trying to forget things about the war. I was lucky that my friends picked me up, took me home, threw me into the shower and got me cleaned up. That brought me to my senses, and I made a vow to myself after that to get my act together. I stopped drinking and I started speaking to various medical people about my problems. I needed help along the way to talk about things and accept things, and I got it.

I was lucky that the United States, unlike many other countries, has a Veterans Health Administration with its own hospitals that were staffed by medical personnel and combat veterans who really understood what I had been through. They were helpful and sympathetic about the brutality of war, and could be very descriptive in talking about war, the uselessness of war and the damage that is done in war. They taught me to put things into perspective. Rather than taking on the guilt for the lives I had taken, I needed really to stop and think, and learn to forgive myself for doing what had needed to be done.

After I had received some help, I took Dr Race's advice and set about getting an education so I could concentrate on a career, making myself a useful, productive person. I went to the Curtis Evening High School on Staten Island to get a registered high school diploma so that I could go to university. It wasn't all that easy at first but I was determined and stuck at it.

To help pay for it all I started my own little car wash and chauffeur business. Through my association with Dr Race I was aware of this big office building on Staten Island where many wealthy doctors worked, and I saw an opportunity. When they came into the parking lot I had a little thing going where I would clean the cars and polish them. I would also drive them to the New York ferry and bring their cars back when they were going over to Manhattan, returning later when they needed picking up.

Earning my high school diploma took nearly four years, night after night, including the summers. I often thought about Trix and The Greek but I didn't have any contact details for them and didn't have the time to try to find them.

After getting my diploma I was accepted by Purdue University in West Lafayette, Indiana. I put my trunk in my little car, which the mechanic dad of one of my friends had done his best to make roadworthy, and I drove across Staten Island, through New Jersey, Pennsylvania and several other states across to Indiana. It was quite a journey and took me several days. At one point I was so tired I pulled into this parking lot for a rest, and as I climbed out I noticed that my driver's side tyre was flat. As I stared at it in frustration there were these guys standing around watching me.

They said, 'What's happening, buddy?'

I said, 'Look at that bloody flat tyre.' I must have looked as exhausted and frustrated as I felt.

'Where are you coming from?' they asked.

I said, 'New York.'

One of the guys said, 'Don't worry about it, just give me the keys and go and get yourself a cup of coffee.'

I headed off across the road to the coffee shop, and when I came back the tyre had been fixed and the keys were on the dashboard along with a note that said, 'GI, take care, have a good life.'

I will never forget that act of random kindness. I wasn't in uniform then but with my age and bearing, people just assumed I was ex-army. During my second year at university I got hitched to my first wife, Patricia. Despite my own childhood experiences I wanted to get married and settle down. We first met in Indianapolis at some social gathering, we got to know each other and then I met her family. It just felt right and we got married and ended up with four children, Colleen, Terry, Eddie and Thomas.

I am proud to say I eventually graduated with a degree in clinical psychology with honours. It was quite a milestone for the Guard family. After graduation I was asked to join the university staff; I accepted. Life was finally pretty good for my family and me at long last. While the pay wasn't in the Rockefeller league it was considerably more than I could ever have imagined earning when I was growing up in the slums of Swansea.

I worked at the university for around three years and then I had the opportunity to work in Saudi Arabia, in manpower development with the Arabian American Oil Company (ARAMCO). For me, it was a happy time spent in a wonderful country; there was none of the tension and terror that you see tearing the world apart today and the Saudi people were very welcoming and friendly.

While I was in Saudi Arabia I had the opportunity to take a couple of weeks' vacation and head back to Swansea to see my parents and the rest of the family. While there I happened to run into Mr Hopkins, who ran the Swansea Boys' Club when I was a kid. We gave each other a big hug. It was just great to see him. Then I asked if Mrs Aeron Thomas was still alive. He said yes and so I asked if he knew her address and he gave it to me.

The following day I drove down to her place in the seaside village of Mumbles, west of Swansea, and knocked on the door. She had always been a very impressive lady, and that had not changed. She opened her door and looked at me, and asked, 'May I help you?'

I said, 'Mrs Aeron Thomas, my name is Cliff Guard and I am here to thank you personally for the tremendous impact you have had on my life since I was a boy.'

It was a beautiful afternoon and she had a bench in her garden so we sat down and talked for an hour or so. It gave me the opportunity to express my very deep and sincere appreciation, not just for myself but also to a lot of other very poor boys she had helped.

She asked, 'What are you doing with your life now?'

I said, 'Well, I got an education and I'm a clinical psychologist.'

She said, 'Well, good on you.'

I told her a lot of it was down to the way she had helped us when we were young. She asked me about the other boys and then she shook my hand and gave me a hug and we said our goodbyes. That was the last time I saw her, but she is a lady that I will never forget.

*

I stayed in Saudi Arabia for around three years before the time came to head back to the United States where I had been offered a job working with the Indiana State Prison. However, before flying back to the States I decided to see a bit of Europe—this time at a more leisurely pace. I hired a car in Rome and drove my family around northern Italy before heading into Germany where I went back to Darmstadt. I went and looked up that family I had befriended. The old fella and his wife were still alive and he thanked me profusely for what I had done for him and his family. We had a nice talk. His daughter had married her German soldier and was doing well. We had a lovely reunion, and after all the horrors of the war, it felt good to know I had made a difference to this family.

While working at the prison I managed to track down my old buddy Trix. He had settled back home in Pennsylvania and immersed himself in family life, vowing never to venture out into the big bad world again. He told me that he had heard from The Greek and we chatted a little about that. The Greek wasn't working, there wasn't much work around at the time with all the GIs having returned from around the globe, but he said he would try to make it down to Pennsylvania to meet up with him and his family. I managed to do just that a few months later but The Greek never turned up.

It sure was great to see Trix again; it must have been the first time in around ten years. I was very busy when I got back to the States and we were both pulling our lives together and moving forward. At this point, we were both married with commitments of our own.

After a few years in the prison service I was offered a job with the United States Government at Fort

Benjamin Harrison, in Indiana, in personnel management training. I later worked for the National Highway Institute in Washington DC.

Unfortunately, around about 1981, my marriage to Patty had slowly disintegrated and I found myself alone once more. Despite all the years and the help I had had, I was still all messed up in my head by the repercussions of the war and I just wanted to get off by myself and try to pull myself together; I was very confused. It was a stupid thing to do, to leave my wife and kids, but I did.

I decided to return to Swansea. My kids were all but grown up and America was their home so there was no question of them coming with me. That was mighty hard and not a decision I took lightly but just something that, at the time, I felt I had to do.

I talk to my daughters, Colleen and Terry, at least twice a week. My oldest son, Ed, on the other hand, I don't hear from as often, because he was most upset about me leaving home and he hasn't quite gotten over that. I can't blame him because I left them all in a hell of a hole. I love him dearly and wish that we were closer.

Sadly my youngest son, Thom, lost his life in a car accident a few years back and has left a hole in my life that will never right itself.

*

I can't say enough about the United States and all the great things it has done for me. America gave me opportunities to better myself that would never have been available to me in Wales. It gave me an education, paid for my college and professional training, gave me a good job and a family, overall a good life. However, I felt a longing for my homeland, and knew it was time to head back home across the pond.

Chapter 16

Retirement and Reflection

Putting distance between myself and my old life helped some and it felt good to walk around my old town once more. It echoed with so many childhood memories. But as good as it was being back home I soon realised that having too much time on your hands is not a good thing when you are trying to escape your thoughts, as I was.

Fortunately I was offered a job working with an alcohol and drug advice centre in Swansea. The role, counselling drug and alcohol addicts, allowed me to further my interest in psychology while interacting with and helping people. It helped me feel as though I was doing some good and giving something back to Swansea. Then something else happened that helped me move on with my life; I met Maggie, my second wife. To be honest with you, meeting Maggie was one of the luckiest breaks of my life; not only is she the love of my life, she is my best buddy.

*

Time and life continued to come between myself, Trix and The Greek but they were in my thoughts more than ever and I really began to miss them—most old folks will tell you that you tend to get more and more retrospective as you near the end.

Then, in early 2002, I had a call from a gentleman in Illinois by the name of Olson, who wrote for *The American Legion* magazine. He advised me that the 3rd Armored Division Veterans' Association were holding a reunion and invited me along. I got in touch with Trix—there still wasn't any news from The Greek—and confirmed that we were coming and arranged to meet up in Pennsylvania. We flew out and stayed with my daughter in Virginia before meeting up with Trix and his family. Now I had bought a new hat for this occasion and, by a twist of fate, when I walked in and spotted my old buddy sitting there, he was wearing the exact same hat. We had a good laugh at that.

He looked up at me and said, 'Good God, if it isn't Limey!' It was the first time we had met since way back when I was working in the prison service and had taken my family up to see him in Pennsylvania.

As we talked he asked, 'Hey, Limey, where's my damned hundred dollars?'

I said, 'What are you talking about?'

He said, 'When you went to that city in France I gave you a big wad of my money and never got it back.'

'That was our money,' I said. 'Anyway, I told you, I

put it in the mail. It takes a long time to arrive from Germany.'

A handful of years later, in 2009, Maggie and my oldest daughter, Terry, with the help of some lottery funding, arranged for me to go back to where it all really began, Omaha Beach in Normandy. I couldn't face it before but felt I owed it to my buddies who had not made it home to go and pay my final respects.

We took a walk along the top of the beach and found that bastard pillbox which had taken so many of the guys out. I cannot put into words the feelings of devastation and loss that I felt as I stood there knowing all that had gone on so many years ago. A rush of memories came back about what had gone on around that beach and amongst the hedgerows; the guns may have long since fallen silent but they still echoed in my ears that day.

I was able to hold it together until I went up to see the graves. There were a lot of people at the cemetery; it's a beautiful well-cared-for place, and the staff there were helpful and immensely respectful of our fallen comrades. Some of the areas had been cordoned off in preparation for the upcoming D-Day services, and there was a lady directing people around. When I spoke to her and told her who I was and where I had fought, she took me past the ropes to where some of my buddies were at rest. Looking at their graves I got quite emotional. I had wet eyes, as I recall.

As I was leaving I turned and gave a final salute. Later we went to the town of Saint-Lô, which had been totally rebuilt. We went inside this café and an old woman there saw my medals and came over to speak to us; it turned out she had been one of those liberated by the Americans and she told me to wait there. She went out and came back with the mayor and a bunch of other folk and they were all kissing my cheeks and hugging me.

*

The trip back to Omaha Beach had made me determined to do more to keep in touch with Trix and to step up my efforts to find The Greek, who I hadn't seen since Germany. As it happened, I heard from Trix's daughter shortly afterwards. She got in touch with me but it wasn't good news. She called to say her father was suffering from advanced Parkinson's disease and was in a nursing home. She invited me out to visit but warned me not to expect too much, and that he might not even know me.

Maggie and I flew out to the States and made our way to Pennsylvania and found ourselves at the nursing home where Trix was now living. I was led into this room and saw my old buddy looking quite feeble and slumped forward in a wheelchair. My heart sank. Then he sensed my presence and looked up and said, 'Limey, you sonofabitch, it's good to see ya. Where's that hundred dollars you owe me?'

I said, 'I mailed it to you back in 1945.'

We both had a good laugh, and the years just melted away.

*

After I returned to Swansea I again tried my damnedest to look up The Greek but met a brick wall at every turn. Then along came a moment of serendipity, which may appear to have come right out of a Hollywood movie, but it happened nonetheless. One October day in 2010 Maggie overheard some American voices discussing a menu outside one of Mumbles' many restaurants.

Now Maggie being Maggie, she waded right in and started up a conversation with them. After determining that they were Americans on vacation, she insisted they come upstairs to our flat and meet her husband who had served in the US Armed Forces. Imagine my surprise to walk into our living room and find these two big Yanks and their wives having tea with my wife.

One of the couples, Darin and Carol Lynn Evans, turned out to be from Spring Lake, Michigan. When I heard that, I started telling them all about my old buddy The Greek and how I had lost track but knew that he probably lived somewhere in their state. Then a miracle happened on July 21. Carol was headed to the library, ready to try some new websites when, on a whim, she decided to look in the Muskegon-North Ottawa phonebook.

'How many Kallases can there be in Michigan?' she asked herself.

There was only one listed locally: S Kallas in Muskegon.

She punched the numbers into her phone. Maybe someone knew someone, she hoped, and told the woman who answered the phone why she was calling and asked if she happened to know a man called Henry Kallas.

'I'm his wife,' Shirley Kallas said. And before Carol Lynn could say anything more, Shirley was talking about Limey and Trix and The Greek.

Sadly, bad news followed. The last thing I had said to The Greek, back in Germany, was that I would look him up one day. It had taken the next sixty-six years to make good on my promise—and then, as life would have it, I was too late. The Greek was already gone, dead many years. I was devastated.

Despite hearing the sad news, Maggie and I determined to fly out to the United States and meet Shirley. When we met she put her hands on my face and said: 'Limey, my God. To think I've met Limey. Finally.' There were tears streaming down her face. 'There, there,' I said, putting my arm around her, 'the important thing is we've met now.' There wasn't a dry eye in the room.

She told me that many, many times The Greek would tell her about Limey and Trix. She said, 'He told me about when you got wounded and he told me about when he himself got wounded.' He used to talk about different situations we were in. He spoke about the war a lot but it was always in reference to us three plus a number of our other buddies. It was ever present, our relationship, that's the way it was.

She then introduced me to a good-looking young fella who turned out to be The Greek's grandson. I made a point of telling him, 'Your granddaddy was an exceptional soldier. He was one of the best; someone you could always rely on.'

*

It's right and proper that people take time to remember the fallen and to reflect on their sacrifice and I have spent many occasions selling poppies for the Royal British Legion in the entrance of the very same Swansea market I once used to liberate food from as a child.

Around 2010 I was given the opportunity to pay respect to my fallen buddies when I was invited to lay a wreath, dedicated to the US 1st Army, up in London on Armistice Day. There was a big parade of former servicemen and women who marched from Whitehall to the Cenotaph. The Queen and other dignitaries laid their wreaths, and the parade marched past them afterwards.

Back in the United States I heard that the Stars and Stripes had been flown over the Pentagon in my name.

It's something that is done for different people each day and as it so happened my turn came on Memorial Day in 2013. This was precipitated by close friends of the family, Dan and Carl Keslar, who were aware of my story and wanted to mark the occasion. Afterwards, they brought the flag over to Wales and presented it to me. It was quite touching for them to do this, and very much appreciated.

Then, in June 2013, Maggie and I were invited to a garden party at Buckingham Palace. A letter had landed on my doorstep inviting us to the party, which coincided with the sixty-ninth anniversary of the D Day landings. Maggie bought a new hat and we made our way to London and found ourselves in the grounds of the palace surrounded by hundreds of people in their finery. We were enjoying sandwiches on the immaculate lawns when this important looking guy, he seemed ex-military himself, came up to me and said, 'Excuse me, are you Clifford Guard?' I said, 'Yes, Sir.'

'Do you mind coming with me,' he replied.

He led us towards an area below the balcony overlooking the gardens and stood us in a small line and after a while Her Majesty made her way towards us ... I was about to meet the Queen!

When I was a boy the class system was pretty much at its height, with the lords and ladies and gentry, and never in my wildest dreams would I have said that I would meet the Queen one day. I remember as a kid standing outside a theatre on High Street in Swansea. There was some premiere going on in there, and Mrs Aeron Thomas and all the gentry showed up. I was stood there looking at all these people in their finery and lovely cars, and I thought to myself: isn't that something. Mrs Aeron Thomas smiled over at me and said, 'Hello, Clifford' and I thought to myself, 'That's very nice of her.' I wonder what she would have made of me standing on those manicured lawns at Buckingham Palace waiting to meet the Queen?

When I look back I don't think my parents would have been able to take it all in either, they just wouldn't. It is unbelievable that the Queen would be giving their son Clifford Guard an audience.

When she approached us, I shook her hand and she said something but I didn't quite catch it.

I said, 'Mam, I ain't picking you up too good, I'm kind of deaf.'

She looked at me and smiled and said, 'I'm having the same problem.'

Then Maggie explained to her that as a little child she read about her driving an ambulance during the war. The Queen smiled and said, 'Fancy you remembering that from all those years ago.'

Then she focussed on me and said, 'I understand that you landed on Omaha Beach.'

I said, 'Yes, Mam, on June 23.'

She said, 'Wasn't Omaha American?'

I said, 'Yes, Mam. I'm a Swansea boy but I thought the Americans could do with a hand.' And she gave a little chuckle. I went on to tell her about my service in the British Merchant Marine, and how I had been in the supply convoys before ending up in America where I joined the US Army. She appeared genuinely interested in hearing all about this and how I ended up in Normandy.

*

I was brought back to earth on the way home from that trip to London when I received news that Trix had passed away.

Having read this far you know how close we were—I loved him as a brother—so all I will say here is what I said in his funeral service. Being too damned old myself to fly back I wrote a letter that my daughter, Terry, read out during the service.

> *Trix,*
>
> *I got the news about your passing away while I was travelling by train back from London. It floored me. It brought a flood of memories of the time we served in the Army in the early 1940's—you, me and The Greek, The Three Musketeers.*
>
> *We certainly were one for all and all for one.*
>
> *I am alive today because of you and The Greek's bravery*

in the many fierce, constant battles we fought in throughout Europe.

The three of us, like so many of our buddies, went through hell and back, that's for sure.

Omaha and the Battle of the Bulge were particularly nasty. How we got through it all is beyond me. But on the lighter side, Trix, the most memorable thoughts I have is when you got your first stripes. You looked at me and The Greek and said, 'You guys get me a cup of Java, I'm the boss now,' as you pointed to the top of your arm.

We told you to bugger off. To which you laughed and said, 'I'm only joking.'

Of course we knew it.

But Trix, I think the nicest time the three of us had was listening to Glenn Miller in that dance hall in Weymouth a few nights before we left for Omaha Beach. We talked about it for months afterwards.

Well, I miss you two guys, there's no doubt about it. Take care of each other.

By the way, when I see ya I will be sure to pay ya the hundred dollars I borrowed from you Trix in 1945. I did tell you a long time ago that it was in the mail but I was lying!

Limey
June 6, 2013

Trix is buried up on a hill not too far from where he lived in Pennsylvania. He took me up there once to show me where he wanted to be laid to rest; it's a peaceful and fitting place for such a fine soldier, family man and friend. The Greek rests in Michigan. Both of them had good military send-offs, which is no less than they deserved.

As for my final resting place, I consider myself a Welsh-American and when my time comes I will be cremated in Swansea and my ashes will cross the ocean one last time to be interred in Arlington Cemetery in Virginia. It's the national cemetery for military guys who have done their bit and it's close to where my kids are. It's well kept and it's all military, so I will be amongst my buddies.

*

Time went on and in the summer of 2015, I was invited to Westminster Abbey for a special Victory in Europe Day celebration where little ole Limey got to meet David Cameron, the British Prime Minister.

Then, another honour came my way in the summer of 2018 when I was invited to the US Embassy in London to be awarded the Legion of Honour from the French Government. Some years back the French decided to give all those who played a part in helping liberate their country during the Second World War their highest honour. It was quite an occasion to gather there with my close family and friends and to receive that medal and I made damn sure that I made it clear I accepted it on behalf of my buddies. You never let go of that kind of friendship forged through life and death situations; it's always very close. As I say, many times, if it had not been for The Greek and Trix and my other buddies, I would not be here today, period.

I've heard the expression that we were the Great Generation, and it's difficult for me to put that into perspective in terms of what it meant. I don't see us as anything special. We were a group of men going into a situation that we knew absolutely nothing about. We just did what was right for our country. I saw us as being counted when the time came to be counted.

Some people like to call us heroes: no sir, not in any sense of the word. The heroes didn't come back. It's nice for people to think that way, and they are being kind and generous, but I lost quite a few of my buddies and they are the heroes.

None of the guys that I knew, tankers, engineers, infantry, what have you, ever thought that we were in any way heroes or outstanding soldiers. Those kind of feelings did not come to me or my mates, as far as I can remember. What I do remember, and it's very strong in my mind even at the age of ninety-six, is the fact that we agreed that we would go into Europe and get the job done, to take care of the German war machine. Keep in mind, when I saw my buddies being hurt, wounded and killed, that had an impact on me to get in there and do the worst I could to these bastards when the opportunity presented itself; and that opportunity was pretty much there twenty-four hours a day, seven days a week.

It is also important for me to categorically state that there is absolutely no glory in combat. I never ever, not even for a moment, felt glory. I only felt that I had a job to do and that I was going to do it to the best of my ability. I do remember that when I landed on Omaha Beach I said to myself, 'Okay, you bastards, I'm here and I'm gonna have a shot at ya.' When I looked around at all my buddies, they were doing the same thing. Did I take chances? Yes, I did. Foolish? Yes, I was. I'm amazed today that I'm still here in good enough health to be writing this book.

Sometimes I ask myself if it has all been worthwhile, when I survey the world today and think back to the numbers of young men who died alongside me, giving their lives for a principle called democracy. I would say it has been worthwhile in certain areas but I still think we have a lot to learn from the war; for a start, we need to be more respectful of each other, more understanding and, above all, be more helpful to each other. We have to look to being kind and helpful to other people as we go through life; it's extremely important and is what I have always tried to do.

*

I feel my life is closing now and I do look back on what I've accomplished. I feel that I have done some things in my life that I couldn't have if I had stayed in Wales. In all honesty, it was the United States of America that really shaped my life. It provided the opportunities and I took the opportunities and I feel a sense of satisfaction with what I was able to accomplish. I'm not saying it's any great thing, but we are put on this earth to do something with our life that's constructive and useful and in my closing years I feel as though I have done that.

I have a few regrets; I wish I could have been a better family man. Anyone can be a father, that's just a biological thing, but I feel that I could have accomplished more being a dad, perhaps being closer to my children when I was a young man.

As for death, I think everyone, almost without exception, thinks about eventualities in their life when they get enough years on their shoulders. Death is a very final thing and everybody comes to terms with it in their own way. I have said many times, death is an ending process and it doesn't scare me one bit. When you analyse it, the moment you are born, you are born to die. If you can look at death as the final chapter gracefully and accept it for what it is, the finality of things, then I'm okay with it and not scared of the final moments of leaving this world and moving into whatever is on the other side. Somehow, I know for sure that I will meet up with my buddies again.

Real Stories

'The word "uncensored" reminds me of the time I first became aware of Richards' talents as a writer. It was in trenches, two days after the Battle of Loos, in September, 1915.'
Robert Graves

Old Soldiers Never Die
FRANK RICHARDS

'...a remarkable and fascinating account.'
BBC

Old Soldier Sahib
FRANK RICHARDS

GEORGE
BRINLEY
EVANS

where the
flying fishes play

THE
SONGBIRD
IS SINGING
SCENES FROM A WELSH
CHILDHOOD IN THE 1920S
BY **ALUN TREVOR**

PARTHIAN

www.parthianbooks.com

JOHN MARTIN

OVER

BERLIN

A MIRACULOUS TRUE-LIFE SECOND WORLD WAR SURVIVAL STORY

N°1 BEST-SELLER